REFLECTING ON
JANE EYRE

HEROINES?

Certain fictional women have become part of western mythology. They are the stars of novels, films, radio and TV programmes, which have caught the imagination of generations of women. What is the secret of their magnetism?

This new feminist series about literary heroines investigates their lasting appeal. Each writer explores her chosen heroine's relationships with other characters in the novel, with her own author, with readers past and present, and lastly with herself. These characters all touch chords of reality for us. By their very 'ordinariness' they demonstrate that, in the most general feminist sense, all women are heroines.

For general readers as well as students, these concise, elegantly-written books will delight all lovers – and even haters – of the original classics.

Titles in the series include:

Mary Evans *Reflecting on Anna Karenina*

Pat Macpherson *Reflecting on Jane Eyre*

Rebecca O'Rourke *Reflecting on The Well of Loneliness*

PAT MACPHERSON

REFLECTING ON JANE EYRE

ROUTLEDGE
London and New York

First published in 1989
by Routledge
11 New Fetter Lane, London EC4P 4EE

Simultaneously published in the USA and Canada
by Routledge
a division of Routledge, Chapman and Hall Inc.
29 West 35th Street, New York, NY 10001

© 1989 Pat Macpherson

Typeset by Witwell Ltd, Southport
Printed in Great Britain
by Cox & Wyman Ltd, Reading

British Library Cataloguing in Publication Data

Macpherson, Pat, *1951- .*
Reflecting on Jane Eyre. — (Heroines).
1. Fiction in English. Brontë, Charlotte.
Jane Eyre — Critical studies
I. Title   II. Series
823'.8

ISBN 0-415-01787-4

Library of Congress Cataloging in Publication Data

Macpherson, Pat, 1951- .
Jane Eyre/Pat Macpherson.
p. cm. — (Heroines?)
1. Brontë, Charlotte, 1816-1855. Jane Eyre. 2. Feminism and
literature. 3. Heroines in literature. 4. Women in literature.
I. Title. II. Series.
PR4167. J5M33 1989
823'.8—dc19   89-6033
CIP
ISBN 0-415-01787-4

CONTENTS

Acknowledgements   vii

Introduction   ix

Chapter One: Portrait of a Governess, Disconnected, Poor,
  and Plain   1

Chapter Two: Wild Nights   10
  1. Courtship Part One: Taming Female Desire   22
  2. Courtship Part Two: Taming Male Demand   38

Chapter Three: Heavenly Father   59

Chapter Four: From Bad Girl to Good Woman   87
  1. Gateshead: Woman's Influence   91
  2. Lowood: The Power of Women's Education   95
  3. Thornfield: Romance and Romantics Revised   99
  4. Moor House: Evangelicism for Women   109
  5. Ferndean: Jane's Household   115

Bibliography   119

IN MEMORY OF MY PARENTS

ACKNOWLEDGEMENTS

F RIENDS and family, and colleagues and students at Germantown Friends School in Philadelphia, by asking how the book was going and when they could read it, held me fully accountable to audience. *Jane Eyre* is for – and because of – them.

Academia, in my 'secondary' relationship to it as a high school teacher, gave me the feminist scholarship, the fellow students and professors, and the structure to study *Jane Eyre* formally. I first wrote on feminist critical readings of *Jane Eyre* for Ann Beuf's National Endowment for the Humanities Institute in Women's Studies for Secondary School Teachers at the University of Pennsylvania in the summer of 1980 and again in 1981–2 for my MA degree in Women's Studies at the University of Kent. At Kent, I heard Mary Evans' paper on *Jane Eyre* and *Middlemarch*, 'Woman the sufferer: the morality of inequality', to which this book owes its fundamental premise. Carol Christ's NEH course for high school teachers on 'Five Victorian novels' at the University of California at Berkeley in the summer of 1984, inspired me to map out Bertha's claim to feminism – my first version of 'Wild nights'. And Carol Gilligan's Laurie Chair seminar on 'Female adolescence' at Rutgers University in the autumn of 1986 reminded me of adolescence as a perspective as well as a process, and authorized me to speak as a teacher and former adolescent. For the ideas, friendships, and feedback on my two papers for the seminar, many thanks to all who were present.

Acknowledgements

For both giving me ideas and listening to my own about *Jane Eyre*, my thanks to Mary Evans, Charlotte Pierce Baker, Joan Countryman, Bronwyn Duffy, and Judy Weightman. For both reading and commenting on drafts of the manuscript, my thanks to Mary Evans, David Gelsanliter, and Kate McLuskie. For editorial support and inspiration, I would like to thank Gill Davies and for library assistance, I would like to thank both Florence Goff and Ann Denlinger at the Bryn Mawr College Library. For word-by-word editing of the entire manuscript, with as much humour as critical edge, I owe Bronwyn Duffy a debt I cannot repay. Finally, by sharing with me 'The Carpenter's Book of Skill and Knowledge', Don Macpherson taught me what I know about construction, design, and craftsmanship and demystified 'Art' with many a fast fart.

INTRODUCTION

I was aged thirteen when I found *Jane Eyre* in my parents'
study, the only cosy room in our formal house. It was the 1943
Random House edition with gothic-looking engravings by
Fritz Eichenberg. First, I read the illustrations – of cold, rich
interiors, of wild passions unleashed – and could not believe
that the story could fulfil the promise of such dreams depicted.
Pictures from childhood, text quite adult: this, then, was my
bridge.

Like Jane, I discovered on the first page that I was an
uncongenial alien who had retreated from the family circle to
read in private. Jane's chafing boredom in the midst of
domestic plenty, and her building excitement in the midst of
stark imaginative realms outlined my own solitary struggle with

the adult world's mysterious meanings and my own uncharted beckoning interior. What haunted our houses?

Dear dead Mr Reed is Jane's first ghost; he had promised to protect her future welfare and then slipped away. Bertha is Jane's second ghost – Rochester's unannounced mad wife haunting Jane's courtship from the attic at Thornfield. I had mysteries, I had ghosts. Why had my parents' once-companionate marriage turned fiery in this strange house? Now it was triangulated with an unspoken third element – perhaps a third gender, unaproned and unbusinesslike. Not father, certainly not mother, a threat to both: 'female desire', unspeakable in 1964, unpresentable in the parlour, but all-too-vociferous in the attic. *The Second Sex* sat by my mother's chair in the living room, loudly proclaiming her objections. A father who could – or would – no longer protect with his absent presence, a mother who had lost her force of gravity and had left the household weightless, floating. Privately, secretly, behind closed doors we politely came undone, while other families, all as unseen and unsaid, did the same. The 'feminine mystique' had lost its power, its purpose, and what looked like sheer anarchy was loosed within my mother. The household's centre did not hold.

This gothic moment of my adolescence was uncannily central, not marginal, to the history of the middle-class family in the mid-1960s in America. Strange and violent dreams – of citizens attacked by police dogs, of first a President assassinated, and then his assassin, as I watched – killed our TV-version of national security. The images outspoke the explanations. Endless replays made a mockery not only of rational commentary, but of all the TV families on other channels still feeding themselves on 'Mom and apple pie'.

Jane Eyre knew this. The text's stern rationality was my salvation. The narrator was not vainly promising but actually demonstrating a fully controlled adult consciousness. Here, then, was the gravity and visualized future so mysteriously absent in my real life. Here was the means for me to comprehend the plot unfolding in my family. Here was my route from windowseat to my own household.

What, then, did my students read in *Jane Eyre* after twenty years of feminism and family revision? What had happened to all my questions about the family and female education, and work and sexuality, and romance and religion and morality? In 1984, feminism framed our reading, and that politicized consciousness and its public forum – the classroom – made all the difference for me from my first isolated reading. Instead of characters and their revealing scenes remaining safe and unprobed in the dream world of my secret reader's space, they were pushed into a high school English class with twenty more-or-less interested juniors, asked pointed questions and sometimes subjected to rude speculations. To what end? I did not want essays treating *Jane Eyre* as a sacrosanct text that it would pay them to pay homage to. Rather, through writing a journal entry after each reading assignment, and by asking irreverent questions myself, I wanted them to discover their own questions as they read, as I, hungrily had found my own embedded there.

Two young women in particular taught me crucial generational differences between us. Esther studied Rochester's terms for romance and St John's for religion, and like Jane looked for the power and the alternative morality with which to revise the double standard of sexual conduct to allow both sexuality and salvation for Jane in the end. Anna, in approving Jane's calm ending after her fiery beginning, argued herself out of passion, conceived of as the threat of tempestuous feelings to the stability and continuity of relationships. Both young women assumed, as I did aged thirteen, that Rochester was a worthy resting place after Jane's wearisome quest. But twenty years of feminism, divorce, and mothers in the labour market had revised Esther's and Anna's expectations of romance and happily ever after. In 1964, I had looked to fiction and romance (and later, to my career) as free space, a real escape from the power relations skewering my family. By 1984, those easy exits were closed. All gender relations and women's work were on the map of power relations, all fictional endings of romantic transcendence made 'corny' by the real lives of real mothers.

Esther and Anna were more sophisticated than I had been in

analysing the terms of Jane's fulfilment as a woman, but just as keen to solve the mysteries of female appetite and household provision. What Esther, Anna, and I shared in *Jane Eyre* was a reading of ourselves, present-to-future, that half-described and half-prescribed our course out of lost girlhood to the resting place of fulfilled womanhood.

Jane at the age of ten looked down the years and knew she could improve on Mrs Reed's 'overupholstered' and 'undersprung' mothering; I myself, at the age of thirteen looked down the years and refused my mother's desperate flirtation with the madwoman in the attic, and fashioned myself as watchful governess; Esther and Anna looked at me, a married feminist twenty years older, and at Jane's final deal with Rochester, and thought: 'It can be done', love and independence, family and career, education and work.

'Her life was a book which she herself seemed to be constructing – trying to make character clear before her, and looking into the ways of destiny' (Uglow, 1987:189), as one of George Eliot's heroines sees it. Can we, at the ages of thirteen or seventeen, write the life as we would the book? The question itself is our enabling female fiction. From real women we learn what 'place' means, the limits of female space and power in the world as it presently is constituted. When my mother tested her place in our household, I saw her, not it, give in. From fiction, we learn how far we might push the limits of our own space and power, redesign, even, the place of education, romance, and religion – as Jane Eyre shows us how to do. This tension between female place and space is the material of domestic feminism, as alive in public debate in Charlotte Brontë's day as in our own. Charlotte Brontë's brilliant achievement is to domesticate the terms of the debate to literal household situations – Jane at Gateshead, Lowood, Thornfield, Moor House, and Ferndean – and to narrate the tension of the debate as a psychosocial drama within Jane Eyre, a struggle between a controlling rationality as a kind of realism, and a gothicized imagination with extraordinary powers of its own.

The powerful, dark lover on his prancing steed, the stern conscientious father with his burning ambitions, the mysterious dark lady announcing large appetites – gothicized, semi-satirized, or fairy-tailored, these figures haunt the psychic terrain between childhood and adulthood. Jane Eyre meets and more than matches their adult social expectations for her, and so wrestles into realism the threatening spectres looming over her psychic landscape. What is adolescence – what is feminism – if not wrestling into realism these figures of command and prohibition, duty and desire? This is the psychosocial stuff of which identity is made, including the exceptionally slippery terms of feminine and feminist identity.

Feminism cannot survive as an adult conversation conducted in the hall outside the high school classroom, while the students waiting for their teacher get louder and more restless and more convinced that the homework can be copied and the grades grubbed without reference to their own real lives and concerns. My reading of *Jane Eyre*, and my feminism, started from the questions of my own adolescence. In identifying with Jane Eyre as the subject, the narrator, the moral agent of her own experience, I practised how to become the nervy heroine, rather than the confused victim, of my own experience.

NOTE

All quotations from *Jane Eyre* are cited by page number immediately following the quotation, and taken from the New American Library edition of 1960.

Chapter One

PORTRAIT OF A GOVERNESS, DISCONNECTED, POOR, AND PLAIN

C HARLOTTE BRONTË'S heroine is a governess, one of the dispossessed middle-class women with no dowry or provider, left virtually to 'beg for their living', tugging at the skirts of more prosperous middle-class families. As M. Jeanne Peterson points out in 'The Victorian governess: status incongruence in family and society' (Peterson, 1972), the governess bore on her humble shoulders many of the incongruences of the middle-class female's situation in the 1840s, most noticeably the fact that while there was scant economic and social provision for unmarried women, there was less propriety in paid employment for a lady. Accounts of the 1840s agree 'there was a sudden increase in the number of gentlewomen without financial support in the years following the Napoleonic wars' (Peterson, 1972:6). 'The great curse of a single female life is its dependency', Charlotte Brontë wrote to a friend in 1848. But, as she also noted, 'the present market for female labour is quite overstocked' (Peters, 1986:276).

The governess was an embarrassing exception to the success of the family as the economic brick of the society – and she was treated as the social embarrassment she was. Falling between the roles of relation, guest, mistress, and servant, she had no place of security; little wonder she was often accused of not knowing her place. As Jane Eyre describes herself in Mrs Reed's eyes, she is 'an uncongenial alien permanently intruded on her own family group' (Brontë 1960:18). The scornful disapproval of such women for being dependent and unmarried implies their own responsibility for their almost illegitimate, certainly orphaned status. 'As one fictional uncle said (in Wilkie Collins' *No Name*) about his two well-bred, genteel, but technically illegitimate nieces, as he robbed them of their inheritance: "Let them, as becomes their birth, gain their bread in situations"' (Peterson, 1972:10). While the governess had little respect or authority in her employer's family or among the servants, she yet had the responsibility of educating the young in the moral and social behaviour of their class. Her own 'education for leisured gentility' was 'prostituted' by her work half-outside the home, Peterson says: 'as a governess she had sold herself as an ornament to display her employer's prestige' (Peterson, 1972:11).

'Be a governess! Better be a slave at once! (Brontë, 1974:245). Mrs Pryor speaks from her own experience in *Shirley*, based all too recognizably on Charlotte Brontë's own governessing slavery in her twenties. As she wrote to her sister Emily in 1839:

> I have striven hard to be pleased with my new situation. . . . The children are constantly with me, and more riotous, perverse, unmanageable cubs never grew. As for correcting them, I soon quickly found that was entirely out of the question: they are to do as they like. A complaint to Mrs Sidgwick brings only black looks upon oneself, and unjust, partial excuses to screen the children. . . . I said in my last letter that Mrs Sidgwick did not know me. I now begin to find that she does not intend to know me, that she cares nothing in the world about me except how to contrive how the greatest possible quantity of labour may be squeezed out of me, and to that end she overwhelms me with oceans of needlework, yards of cambric to hem, muslin nightcaps to make, and, above all things, dolls to dress. I do not think she likes me at all. . . . I see now more clearly than I have ever done before that a private governess has no existence, is not considered as a living and rational being except as connected with the wearisome duties she has to fulfil.
>
> (Peters, 1986:70)

A governess's job was not a solution so much as an alleviation of a women's dependency. It 'was only of very limited use even in maintaining gentle status' (Peterson, 1972:7). Her salary probably sagged at the bottom of the range between £15 and

£100 a year, most likely between £20 and £45. Jane's was £30 at Thornfield, double her teacher's salary at Lowood. Hardly the £150 – 200 necessary to a single person's gentility. Having a job did little to enhance her marriageability; attractiveness in a governess was only a problem, a threat to the family.

Only in fiction lived the possibility and propriety of marrying the boss or his son. The few governess novels written before *Jane Eyre* portray her situation in much more convention – bound terms. Patricia Thomson in her study, *The Victorian Heroine* (1956), cites three such novels. *The Governess* by Lady Blessington (1839), in which:

> The beautiful young heroine, Clara Mordaunt, is left destitute by the bankruptcy and suicide of her father and is forced to seek a post as a governess. In the four situations she fills before she is rescued by an offer of marriage from a lord and a legacy from a relative, she experiences all the miseries peculiar to the governess' lot.
>
> (Thompson, 1956:44)

Bankruptcy and suicide are conventional failings in a Victorian father, beauty and purity quite feminine virtues in a daughter, and a title and marriage offer the best moral recommendations in a husband. In Harriet Martineau's *Deerbrook* (1839), the governess 'is not young enough to fill the heroine's role nor sufficiently ill-treated to be pathetic. She is merely poor, lame, unwell, and independent enough to find a substitute for love and affection in her thoughts, her books and her plain sewing' (Thomson, 1956:44). The two sisters who are the heroines have the beauty, youth, and optimism essential to marriageability. The pot of gold for a heroine was matrimony, 'her only true escape, her one hope of happiness on earth' (Thomson, 1956:41). Elizabeth Sewell's *Amy Herbert* (1844) has a governess for a paragon if not a titled heroine: 'beautiful, shy, religious, high-principled, gentle. But a paragon, it seemed, destined to end her days as a governess in the sunshine of the Herbert family' (Thomson, 1956:46). Her humility perhaps insures her dependence instead of her escape from it – such is the conclusion Jane Eyre seems to have reached at a very early age.

Portrait of a Governess

'One of a tribe of governesses whose especial heritage was submission' (Thomson, 1956:47), Jane Eyre and her contemporary Becky Sharpe in *Vanity Fair* (1847) were rebelliously independent:

> They followed the fashion, set a hundred years earlier, of marrying into their employers' family. They themselves set a new fashion – of considering themselves as women, first, and dependants, second.... *Jane Eyre* was of the two the more revolutionary document, the Magna Charta of governesses.
>
> (Thomson, 1956:46)

For Jane to be disconected and poor, capable and intelligent was no more than her lot as a governess heroine. 'She was bound to be a lady – preferably the daughter of a clergyman' (Thomson, 1956:39) if she followed the real as well as the fictional type. In 1851 there were almost 25,000 governesses in England, all, no doubt, capable novel-readers. Clergymen's daughters would have the education without the dowry that was the governess's special qualification. But Jane is more than capable; she is an overachiever.

As heroine, Jane's first act is to demolish the Victorian verities that childhood, and especially girlhood, are originally innocent, and that innocence is virtue, and goodness is patient humility. She challenges us to identify with her *as a bad girl*, who will not relinquish her criticisms of the conventions with which the Reeds bully her, all 'for her own good' *(15)*.

Jane Eyre has already been cast out of the family circle when we meet her, defined by her own bad nature, told that 'until you can speak pleasantly, remain silent'[9]. Retreating to the windowseat, separated from both the inhospitably drear November day outside and the false and unfulfilling fake-log-fire version of family happiness enacted by the Reeds inside, Jane pulls the red moreen curtain nearly close, and reads. There, like Dr Frankenstein in his laboratory, she sets to work on her ungodly experiment in self-creation, which when quickened with the lightning of her own female imagination, lurches forth to wreak havoc on the households where hypocrisy enslaves discontented little cavillers like Jane Eyre.

Enter John Reed, first of the series of male 'interruptors' of Jane's enabling female fictions. His world is the material world of property, and he owns the book she's reading, and the house – 'or will do in a few years'. His legacy is assumed as male heir, which grants him an authority unquestioned by his widowed mother. He neatly sums up Jane's situation as an unattached bourgeois female: her father left her nothing, she has no money so she has 'no business' with 'a gentlemen's children'; instead of being 'a dependent', she 'ought to beg' for a living *(12–13)*. She has no place in this family structure.

When he says that the book is his, she disputes possession with outrage. Jane's rebellion begins when her face registers scorn and disgust in response to John Reed's ranting at her; he reads it and hits it. Then he throws the book at her – and this, for the first time, causes her to strike back, first through talking back, and when this proves provocative, throught fighting back with her body in a most unfeminine fashion.

Jane strikes back by asserting her right to the privacy of her imaginative world, and by challenging his rights to tyrannical control over the bookshelf and over her. She learns the power of the spoken word, moves beyond self-protection to passionate self-declaration, and defends the world of books and imagination as her claim to authority, over Gateshead's hierarchy in which there rules the first order of censorship: 'Until you can speak pleasantly, remain silent'.

She definitively differentiates herself from the Reeds by speaking instead of being silenced or spoken through, governed by some combination of coercion and complicity: '*Speak* I must: I had been trodden on severely, and *must* turn: but how?' *(38)*. For women, this moment of recognition of one's own authority to interpret one's own experience is almost inevitably transgressive, whether against female duty, propriety, or nature. It has been unspeakable outside the language of feminism. For Jane, and many women, it is the beginning of all moral agency. Once capable of interpreting her situation in her own terms, Jane inadvertently discovers she can speak her difference of view to her cousin John: 'I had drawn parallels [from books] in silence, which I never thought thus to have declared aloud' *(13)*.

Then she sees that she has some power to challenge the authority of John and Mrs Reed and Reverend Brocklehurst by talking back to them, by using their own words against them.

When her aunt summons Reverend Brocklehurst to retrain her at Lowood, she specifies her goal: 'This little girl has not quite the character and disposition I could wish ... I should wish her to be brought up in a manner suiting her prospects, to be made useful, to be kept humble' (35–6). Make her a governess, and rid her of all manners not suiting her position and prospects. Since the family has failed to teach Jane her place, religion and education are expected to complete the job. Brocklehurst's bullying catechism begins: 'Well, Jane Eyre, and are you a good child?' She knows but does not dare say that it was: 'Impossible to reply to this in the affirmative: my little world held a contrary opinion; I was silent' (34). This is her problem with propriety, with religion, with the world so far as she knows it. If goodness is more 'childlike' (9) than her plain questioning, then goodness is a hypocrisy, and piety a cruel weapon against the weak. Jane finds a way to slip Brocklehurst's noose of orthodoxy:

> 'No sight so sad as that of a naughty child, especially a naughty little girl. Do you know where the wicked go after death?'
> 'They go to hell,' was my ready and orthodox answer....
> 'What must you do to avoid it?'
> I deliberated a moment; my answer, when it did come, was objectionable: 'I must keep in good health, and not die.' (34)

Jane reveals her true feelings to Mrs Reed after Brocklehurst has left, challenging her aunt's very morality. She lets loose a self-righteous condemnation that begins with a denial of the charge of deceit laid on Jane, and ends with the countercharge, '*You* are deceitful!' By speaking her mind – her 'little world [which] held a contrary opinion' – she seems to break out of the prison of her aunt's expectations.

> 'I am not deceitful.... People think you a good woman, but you are bad; hard-hearted. *You* are deceitful!'
> Ere I had finished this reply, my soul began to expand, to exult, with the strangest sense of freedom, of triumph, I ever felt.

It seemed as if an invisible bond had burst, and that I had struggled out into unhoped-for liberty....

I was left there alone – winner of the field. It was the hardest battle I had fought, and the first victory I had gained: I stood awhile on the rug, where Mr Brocklehurst had stood, and I enjoyed my conqueror's solitude. (*38–40*)

But the issue of who is the good woman, and who is the bad one, and who is deceitful, is not so tidily solved by plain speaking. Jane may have cowed Mrs Reed and won her release from the prison of Gateshead, but she has made of her own mind:

A ridge of lighted heath, alive, glancing, devouring ... the same ridge, black and blasted after the flames are dead, would have represented as meetly my subsequent condition, when half an hour's silence and reflection had shown me the madness of my conduct, and the dreariness of my hated and hating position.

Something of vengeance I had tasted for the first time; as aromatic wine it seemed, on swallowing, warm and racy: its after-flavour, metallic and corroding, gave me a sensation as if I had been poisoned. Willingly would I now have gone and asked Mrs Reed's pardon; but I knew, partly from experience and partly from instinct, that was the way to make her repulse me with double scorn, thereby reexciting every turbulent impulse of my nature.

I would fain exercise some better faculty than that of fierce speaking; fain find nourishment for some less fiendish feeling than that of sombre indignation. I took a book – some Arabian tales: I sat down and endeavoured to read. I could make no sense of the subject; my own thoughts swam always between me and the page I had usually found fascinating. (*40*)

Now that she is 'free', Jane's passion becomes her own problem, no longer Mrs Reed's. She's in deep waters now if she is unable to summon the 'restraint over passions without which the female character is lost', as John Conolly described the genesis of female insanity in 1849 (Showalter, 1985:48). Already Bertha is lurking somewhere in Jane's attic. Jane is to learn her needed self-control at Lowood, where Helen Burns and Miss Temple cultivate in Jane a 'better faculty than that of fierce speaking', and give her 'nourishment for some less fiendish feeling than that of sombre indignation'. With an educated mind, Jane the governess will be equal to the romantic temptations of Thornfield.

Her righteousness is a terrible swift sword in combat with the Reeds, but not with her own daunting demons inside. Each prison cell of social place and female nature that she finds a way out of seems to have its secret trap door into her own unconscious, into which she tumbles when near 'the hour of triumph'. Female creativity, sensuality, solitude, ambition, achievement, subversion, confrontation, vengeance, anger, discontent, passion – all are claimed by Jane as part of her nature. But before her truth can go marching on, she must wrestle with the monster this makes of her, in the dark alley of her own imagination. And she must learn the social use of the double-edged sword of female purity and piety.

How threatening passion remains for Jane, and how difficult purity is to maintain. At Thornfield she dances out her self-division with Bertha, that giggling ghost, as her partner. At Moor House she scrubs herself down so thoroughly she's in danger of self-erasure. The problem is how to make of purity 'an active force' of moral agency that can enable 'women to exercise moral, and to a certain extent social, control over men' (Evans 1982). Jane's task is to find an alternative to the enduring double standard of morality that sets 'purity' as a passionless and passive 'it', first victimized and then saved. *How to make purity and passion a part of moral agency*: Tricky! This monumental project of redefinition, undertaken by such novels as *Jane Eyre*, is on-going, as I write, within young women coming of age today.

Though novels themselves were about female transgression in their hundred-year history before Charlotte Brontë's moment of writing *Jane Eyre* in 1847, convention had largely limited the plot to courtship, the heroine to beauty and innocence, the temptation to transgression of the rules of propriety in courtship, and the outcome to either reward or punishment. The basic bourgeois economic formula, that purity = (ignorant) innocence = marriageability, remained largely unchallenged, while the delicacies of female self-protection and the subtleties of male interest and assault were endlessly investigated. With a reactionary morality familiar to us today, propriety put skirts around male aggression and strip-teased female victimhood.

Rather than begin with innocence and imperil 'it' pornographically for thousands of pages as did Samuel Richardson in *Pamela* and *Clarissa*, Charlotte Brontë begins with an already fallen female. 'Fallen' is riddled with ironies about what the terms of innocence are and should be for young women. Charlotte Brontë's transgression and triumph in *Jane Eyre* was to include much of the bad girl in her heroine and then redefine and redesign her into a new good woman, and to give gothic expression to all the rest that could *never* be made acceptable. Jane Eyre as heroine and Charlotte Brontë as writer rewrite Victorian Woman into a whole, to include intellect *and* feeling, passion *and* reason, rebellion *and* propriety, transgressive desire *and* virtue.

John Reed's bullying about the terms of literary possession and propriety clarifies that literary territory is being fought over here, yet, in secret, women may already have possessed the volume. The courtship story's coy pseudo-mystery of female desire and the puritanical inevitability of moral judgment on female propriety undergoes serious revision in Charlotte Brontë's capable hands. The *morality* of ten–year–old Jane's claimed territory – where imagination and intellect and passion and judgment are all in play – is what she must learn to articulate, and not just blindly, mutely fight for. *Jane Eyre* shows how the novel itself in the hands of middle-class women readers and writers can be the territory for women's exploration of a morality of desire and power, alternative to the material and sexual double standard of middle-class men.

Chapter Two

WILD NIGHTS

J ANE'S experience as governess at Thornfield is a very dull business until Mr Rochester thunders home and falls off his horse at the sight of her. Their love affair apparently accounts for readers' excitement about the novel, and even Charlotte Brontë's. She wrote the Thornfield chapters without a break, in what Margot Peters calls a 'kind of inspired transport, never stopping until Jane left Rochester, finding herself exhausted and feverish for days afterward' (Peters, 1986:215). For some, a good romance is like a good ride: 'When I had once begun it, I could not lay it down again; – I remember finishing it in two days – my hair standing on end the whole time' (Austen, 1903:79).

But I would argue that it is Bertha, Rochester's mad wife hidden in his attic, who accounts for the novel's underground pull on the reader, a force felt but scarcely seen, running against the current of romantic attraction between Rochester and Jane. Bertha is not introduced to the reader or to Jane until Jane's wedding day *(Chapter 26)*; until then Jane thinks it is the servant Grace Poole who lives and laughs in the attic, pulling midnight tricks on the unsuspecting.

Precisely because Jane remains unconscious of Bertha, the charge of psychic symbolism builds dramatically between the two. For the reader as well as for Jane, conscious identification with Bertha can be all too rationally minimized, but unconscious recognitions create an intimacy that is unsupervised by conscientious commentary, uncaptioned by any social meaning at all.

Charlotte Brontë's plot makes parallels between Jane and Bertha at Thornfield, the one known (by the reader) and rationally knowing, the other unknown (by the reader) and irrationally knowing of some mystery. By juxtaposing these two women, Brontë creates subliminal comparisons, connections, even communications between them, and the reader feels or intimates these as the delicious tension of the gothic, the extraordinarily pleasurable fear called the uncanny.

The uncanny occurs at boundary lines, between the known and the unknown, the real and the unreal, the conventional and the unconventional, the acceptable and the forbidden. Feelings of liberation, fear, and guilt mix at the moment of transgression of some boundary, and at the apprehension of the previously unknown. Transgressive desire breeds guilt, not just about obvious criminality, but guilt about its unconscious potential in all our ghostly unacknowledged feelings, which threaten to overturn, even avenge, our investment in innocence.

The uncanny occurs when the familiar turns odd, the expected never shows up, and the dreaded finally arrives, but in drag. Coming from the edge of vision, unasked and unearthed, the uncanny seems to ghost-walk as if alive and dead at the same time, raising the goosebumps of paradox. The uncanny is an impossible question, promising but never quite delivering all the answers.

Bertha provides all the uncanny that Jane can handle in her quest to understand the mysteries of womanhood, romance, and marriage whilst at Thornfield. Bertha explains readers' intense identification with Jane, particularly young women in Jane's position of considering marriage against the single life. Bringing Bertha out of the closet in discussing *Jane Eyre* makes the subliminal manifest, reveals what is hidden in the course of first reading the novel. By reading the novel 'inside out' we can see how *the uncanny works as a powerful vehicle for the novel's feminism*.

When she is stripped of all mystery (the essence of her symbolic power), Bertha's all-too-prosaic powerlessness stands naked before us. The daughter of a colonial planter and a Creole in Jamaica, Bertha Mason was wedded to the young

Edward Rochester for a dowry of £30,000 negotiated by Rochester's father and older brother. Domestic life with such a dark lady was quite uncivilized, Rochester quickly learned – along with the alarming fact that his mother-in-law was already an imprisoned lunatic, and her daughter's temper was rapidly ripening into full-blown depravity, well-watered as she kept it with her 'intemperate and unchaste habits'. Doctors soon certified Bertha as 'mad – her excesses had prematurely developed the germs of insanity' *(309)* – and the law sealed Rochester's fate: legal responsibility with no divorce. What ten or twenty years in the attic with Grace Poole may have contributed to Bertha's mental health is left to our imagination, as are her feelings and thoughts, if any, about her situation. She utters no intelligible words, has no identifiable humanity left, only animal noises and violent acts. There is nothing more to 'know' about Bertha in the world of the novel; as the uncanny, she exists only in relation to the known: to Rochester's uncovered past and Jane's unconscious present.

Jane's discontent as a governess leads her to Bertha's domain, Thornfield's third story. Indeed, Bertha *is* the novel's 'third story', as Elaine Showalter says in her groundbreaking study, *A Literature of Their Own* (Showalter, 1977:118). With great bursts of gothic implausibility, Bertha disrupts the more conventional stories of Jane's 'pilgrim's progess' and Rochester's 'rake's reform'. She begins with a laugh. 'While I paced softly on, . . . a laugh struck my ear' *(110)*, Jane all unwittingly describes her temptation and fall to that whispering snake in the grass. Jane's restlessness puts her in the deviant and pacing company of the unseen Bertha, where she finds herself virtually impregnated with female desire, as she describes it: 'quickened with all of incident, life, fire, feeling that I desired and had not in my actual existence' *(112)*. Her situation as governess is remarkably like Bertha's as a wife: disinherited, dependent, domesticated, and discontented, fermenting rebellion in a cramped solitary confinement. Jane's unfulfilled life as a single woman, an odd woman, is oddly like Bertha's frenzied imprisonment as surely one of the unhappiest of married women. Bertha's laughing lunacy 'seemed to wake an echo in every lonely chamber'. It certainly raises questions about the nature of marital bliss. Why is this woman laughing? 'It was a curious laugh' Jane notes on first hearing it; 'distinct, formal, mirthless' *(110).*

These two women in Rochester's attic raise the novel's question of female fates in relation to potential male protectors, as Jane subliminally recognizes when she first sees the attic. She thinks of 'some Bluebeard's castle' *(110),* that legendary place where a succession of murdered wives was stored. The contrast between the two women is educational, Jane the potential student to Bertha's experience. Jane's fate is still open, her dreaming anticipatory and perhaps unrealistic, admittedly unschooled, 'a tale that never ended – a tale my imagination created, and narrated continuously' *(112).* As in romance fiction, the desires of life–to–be–lived are all in play. Bertha's fate is sealed, and her real-life tale untold, unknown, and all but over, her laugh more punctuation than narration. Yet still she finds a way to make herself known.

The story of Jane at Thornfield, which is the story of her courtship, is not only haunted by Bertha, but made meaningful by her, unspeaking and unspeakable as she is. Bertha is the mystery that Jane must recognize and demystify in order to understand Rochester's marriage offer, and the nature of marriage itself. Yet Jane's innocence must remain that of a child in protection of her virtue and romance, so she improbably remains oblivious to the adult meaning of Bertha's knowing laugh and the not–so–subtle subtext about the politics and psychology of sexual relations.

It's partly a matter of remaining literal-minded. I'll provide two examples at my own expense. Once, in Boston, as I charged into a magazine store looking for cigarettes, my husband pulled me back and pointed to the sign saying 'Adults only'. Shrugging him off I said, affronted, 'I'm over 21!' and took another literal-minded step before I 'got it'. Then, years later, evidently having retained my capacity for pre-sexual innocence, I was lounging on a bench by a river, bundled against the stiff breeze, sunning myself in the early spring, secure in the bosom of an isolated Victorian town where my parents-in-law had retired. Suddenly a voice called from behind me, 'How you doing?' Startled out of my revery, I saw a man my father's age; could it be one of their friends I had just met? I was saved the social embarrassment by his next question: 'Wanna go for a ride?' I assumed his fatherliness, while he assumed my availability as a publicly loitering woman. As my mental gears ground, shifting from safe girl to unsafe woman, the clutch slipped and I thought: 'I'm being solicited by one of my parents' friends'. No safe places anymore, no safe grandparents. I was feeling safe, in both instances, even though in public, because in Boston I was flanked by two tall men and I was dressed in jeans and a coat, and in the little town I was bundled up and surrounded by the architecture of Victorian family structures. I was free to forget about my body as a public object for look, comment, and harassment, and that freedom evidently returned me to the state of mind of a pre-sexual girl who does not see the assaultive sexual codes behind the 'innocent' phrasing. If female sexuality is publicly read as pornographic, only in privacy and perhaps only in a sexual innocence can young women retain a sense of themselves as safe – meaning not just unassailable, but good, pure and respected. Such literal-minded innocence as Jane Eyre's is not dismissable as Victorian, but remains the place of ultimate security and comfort.

Jane doesn't 'get it' until Rochester is forced to explain it to her when Bertha has been exposed as his wife. Even then, Bertha's possible meanings are never articulated, perhaps never consciously recognized. While at Thornfield, Jane remains the curious child who hears the curious laugh that 'seemed to wake an echo in every lonely chamber; though it originated but in one and I could have pointed out the door whence the accents issued' *(110)*. Precocious, she thinks she knows where it's coming from; sensitive and lonely, she's a chamber in which meaning echoes again and again; stubbornly refusing this self-knowledge, she locates all mystery, knowingness, and preternatural possibilities in the Other.

Bertha plays marital jokes like setting fire to Rochester's bed, biting the hand that feeds her, and pretending to be a vampire during a houseparty charades night. Getting more obvious, she even dresses up in Jane's bridal veil, making ugly faces in Jane's mirror, tearing the veil in two, trampling on it, and then snuffing her candle in Jane's face. What more warning does the poor girl need from Rochester's wife on the night before her wedding?

Unable to figure it out, Jane asks Rochester to tell her whether she was awake or dreaming, and what it all means. 'I don't understand enigmas. I never could guess a riddle in my life' (*199*). With him as her sole source of knowledge, she protects the courtship by remaining impervious to Bertha as a source of meaning – and at the same time to herself as a source of meaning. Jane has everything to learn from Bertha about trickery, especially self-trickery, in courtship, about discontent and suppression and bitterness in marriage, and about the less glamorous motives of Rochester in relation to Bertha and perhaps even to Jane. If Jane doesn't put it together for herself as she needs it, female readers may yet make the connections that appear, perhaps even now, too lunatic to speak without censure or misunderstanding.

From her first intimations of Bertha, when Jane first hears her laugh, Jane's unacceptable – because they are unwomanly – qualities are implicitly linked to Bertha's. In her famous proclamation from the battlements of Thornfield Hall, Jane connects her discontent with thwarted desire and with social disapproval – the very three problems by which Bertha is bound and gagged. And Charlotte Brontë, too: as a writer she shares these bindings and gags with all Victorian women writers. Patsy Stoneman in her study of Elizabeth Gaskell summarizes the dilemma very well: 'It is impossible for Elizabeth Gaskell's female protagonists to speak and act as she thinks rational, humane people should without getting entangled in notions of feminine propriety' (Stoneman, 1987:177).

> Anybody may blame me who likes, when I add further, that, now and then, when I took a walk by myself in the grounds; when I went down to the gates and looked through them along the road; or when, while Adèle played with her nurse, and Mrs. Fairfax

made jellies in the store-room, I climbed the three staircases, raised the trap-door of the attic, and having reached the leads, looked out afar over sequestered field and hill, and along dim sky-line – that then I longed for a power of vision which might overpass that limit; which might reach the busy world, towns, regions full of life I had heard of but never seen that then I desired more of practical experience than I possessed; more of intercourse with my kind, of acquaintance with variety of character, than was here within my reach. I valued what was good in Mrs. Fairfax and what was good in Adèle; but I believed in the existence of other and more vivid kinds of goodness, and what I believed in I wished to behold.

Who blames me? (*112*)

She feebly defends herself by bowing to conventional morality about feminine virtue, saying, 'I valued what was good in Mrs. Fairfax and ... Adèle.' But she wants more. That's her crime, as she knows and protests.

Charlotte Brontë, halting the narrative here at Jane's moment of transgression, asks us to consider who's watching. The gender police are everywhere. Critical judgment is presumed, preceding even Jane's profession of harmless motives in occasional solitary leisure from her duties. The omnipresent and omiscient 'Anybody' is free, if so inclined, to blame Jane. Who is this anybody that the narrator has in mind? Swivelling, she directly addresses us: 'Who blames me?' Readers may well feel their privacy violated by such a question about their motives. 'Having drawn the red moreen curtain nearly close', we believe we are, like Jane, reading her book in Chapter 1, 'shrined in double retirement', seeing but unseen, unapproachable because invisible. With a rude jerk of the curtain, Jane challenges us to answer for our expectations about her behaviour and state of mind.

There is a similar moment in Dorothy Arzner's 1940 feminist film, *Dance, Girl, Dance*, when the good girl ballerina, reduced to dancing in a burlesque by the market for female flesh, suddenly turns in a rage and addresses her male audience's exploitative expectations of her. 'We're paid to pretend you're not out there', she says, 'but that doesn't mean we don't see and reject what your image of us makes you – not us – into. Look at how you see', she challenges, 'before assigning to us the "fallen natures".'

What is appropriate for a governess? For a female autobiographer? And, behind these two women, for a novelist with a purposely genderless pseudonym, Currer Bell? In this passage, Jane anticipates criticism of a particular kind: of herself as a woman, and her answer to this criticism defends women generally, which would include the line of women behind Jane the governess: Jane the narrator, and Currer Bell's hidden writer, Charlotte Brontë, anticipating critics' criticism.

The criticism that the novel *Jane Eyre* did receive in 1847, and the heroine, and Currer Bell, and later when the author was known to be Charlotte Brontë, often stretches to condemn all these women together in the crime of gender transgression. This is not coincidence but convention, Elaine Showalter says: '"The staple of Victorian periodical reviewing" was categorisation according to gender – "sentiment, refinement and tact" for women and "power ... learning ... experience" for men' (Stoneman, 1987: 3).

The anonymous reviewer in the *Christian Remembrancer* in June 1848, Miss Anne Mozley, explains what is unfeminine about depicting Jane Eyre's experiences:

> a book more unfeminine, both in its excellences and its defects, it would be hard to find in the annals of female authorship. Throughout there is a masculine power, breadth and shrewdness, combined with masculine hardness, coarseness, and freedom of expression. Slang is not rare. The humour is frequently produced by the use of Scripture, at which one is rather sorry to have smiled. The love-scenes glow with a fire as fierce as that of Sappho, and somewhat more fulginous. ... If the authoress has not been like her heroine ... at all events we fear she is one to whom the world has not been kind. And assuredly, never was unkindness more cordially repaid. Never was there a better hater.
>
> (Peters, 1986: 205)

According to these standards of femininity, Jane's first boldness is to speak at all. Overleaping the obstacle, grammatically anyway, she boldly persists, she adds further: she specifies her desires with what one might call masculine freedom of expression. And she claims a desire for vision and experience that one might also call masculine in its power, breadth, and shrewdness. Once, twice, thrice, Jane transgresses gender boundaries. Our theme is female transgressive desire.

In the famous feminist speech that follows, the narrator moves from a defence of her individual case to a moral argument for women's right to 'seek to do more or learn more than custom has pronounced necessary for their sex'.

> Who blames me? Many, no doubt; and I shall be called discontented. I could not help it: the restlessness was in my nature; it agitated me to pain sometimes. Then my sole relief was to walk along the corridor of the third story, backwards and forwards, safe in the silence and solitude of the spot, and allow my mind's eye to dwell on whatever bright visions rose before it – and, certainly, they were many and glowing; to let my heart be heaved by the exultant movement, which, while it swelled it in trouble, expanded it with life; and, best of all, to open my inward ear to a tale that was never ended – a tale my imagination created, and narrated continuously; quickened with all of incident, life, fire, feeling, that I desired and had not in my actual existence.
>
> It is in vain to say human beings ought to be satisfied with tranquillity: they must have action; and they will make it if they cannot find it. Millions are condemned to a stiller doom than mine, and millions are in silent revolt against their lot. Nobody knows how many rebellions besides political rebellions ferment in the masses of life which people earth. Women are supposed to be very calm generally; but women feel just as men feel; they need exercise for their faculties, and a field for their efforts as much as their brothers do; they suffer from too rigid a constraint, too absolute a stagnation, precisely as men would suffer; and it is narrow-minded in their more privileged fellow-creatures to say that they ought to confine themselves to making puddings and knitting stockings, to playing on the piano and embroidering bags. It is thoughtless to condemn them, or laugh at them, if they seek to do more or learn more than custom has pronounced necessary for their sex. (*112–13*)

Her most radical claim is that 'the restlessness was in my nature; it agitated me to pain sometimes'. On behalf of all women 'in silent revolt against their lot', she disputes the very reality of the Victorian ideal of womanhood, the selfless angel of tranquillity, by claiming it is not her nature, not women's nature at all; rather, 'women feel just as men feel'. In addition, a very radical process is suggested by the sequence of paragraphs: the first about discontent with women's lot, the second about the provocative power of fiction-making, the third about a desiring female nature that needs exercise and a more public field for efforts.

And third, the fact that Jane and Bertha share these three unfeminine deviancies (and so do the reader and writer of the novel) raises a question about what Jane and Bertha might see in each other if they met. The novel separates the two women as society does; they are not on speaking terms. The 'pure' must stop her ears to the siren song of the 'fallen'; reason is only tempted into darkness by desire. But Jane's and Bertha's pacing communion here restlessly recasts the question: What *is* unacceptable about each woman's right to reason *and* desire? Cora Kaplan (1986) examines the question historically in her essays, 'Wild Nights' (from Emily Dickinson's poem *Were I with thee/Wild nights should be/our luxury*) and 'Pandora's Box'. By so casting Jane and Bertha, Brontë dramatizes a ghost still haunting feminists today: 'The *longing* to close the splits that characterize femininity – splits between reason and desire, autonomy and dependent security, psychic and social identity' (Kaplan, 1986: 154). To explain the mystery, Jane tries to fathom the chasm between Grace Poole's staid and silent appearance, propriety itself, and her overheard eccentric murmurs, the oddity of the unseen Other.

> When thus alone, I not unfrequently heard Grace Poole's laugh; the same peal, the same low, slow ha! ha! which, when first heard, had thrilled me: I heard, too, her eccentric murmurs; stranger than her laugh. There were days when she was quite silent; but there were others when I could not account for the sounds she made. Sometimes I saw her: she would come out of her room.... Her appearance always acted as a damper to the curiosity raised by her oral oddities: hard-featured and staid, she had no point to which interest could attach. I made some

attempts to draw her into conversation, but she seemed a person
of few words; a monosyllabic reply usually cut short every effort
of that sort. (*113*)

Bertha appears here in the text at the height of Jane's desire and
passionate feminist self-declaration, her eccentric oral oddities a
response to Jane's. Jane acts as the rational arguer for women's
rights in this passage, while Bertha, the irrational and unspeakable version of feminism, can only laugh in punctuation for
Jane's claim. Uncannily, Bertha speaks for Jane too, as the
asocial energy of her female imagination. The eroticism of their
similar solitary states is palpable: 'Best of all, to open my
inward ear to a tale that was never ended ... quickened with all
of incident, life, fire, feeling, that I desired and had not in my
actual existence' (*112*). Desire is then dampened by Grace
'policeman' Poole, that 'set, square-made' figure of propriety
and self-control. If the voice of Bertha arouses Jane's curiosity,
the appearance of Grace Poole is enough to thwart it: 'Hard-
featured and staid, she had no point to which interest could
attach' (*112*). 'Any apparition less romantic or less ghostly
could scarcely be conceived' (*110*). Bertha erupts, Grace closes
her off, and Jane's psychic struggle is given graphic literary
expression by this tension between vibrant preternatural gothic
possibility and unromantic, even downright dull domestic
realism.

As a governess, Jane has unsuccessfully dispelled passion; it
has even turned to anger and anxiety at the constricted terms of
her life, work, and identity. Bertha obviously enacts what Jane
feels and cannot find a place for: 'hunger, rebellion and rage'.
Yet given the real social world of Thornfield, the nursery and
the storeroom and the parlour, there *is* no place for anything
but 'a placid-tempered, kind-natured woman, of competent
education and average intelligence' (*111*), as Jane tactfully
describes Mrs. Fairfax. 'A truly refined mind', says Mrs General
in *Little Dorrit*, 'will seem to be ignorant of the existence of
anything that is not perfectly proper, placid, and pleasant'
(Houghton, 1957: 419). With her double burden of Bertha and
refinement, Jane staggers down from the attic to resume her
ill-fitting identity as girl-governess.

Dickens – as a man – can afford to mock Mrs General's way of handling the constraints of female propriety, because he does not have to anaesthetize passion to preserve purity, as a woman must appear to do. He would be the first to jump on Mrs General if she weren't the proper, placid, and pleasant angel mother of his dreams. None the less, his caricature dramatizes the effortful and ridiculously unnatural methods necessary for successful self-repression, as well as the tragedy of self-division and self-deceit that results.

What Jane leaves locked away is our beloved 'madwoman in the attic', Sandra Gilbert and Susan Gubar's name for the archetypal feminist rebel against patriarchy. In my reading, Bertha represents that species of female power and desire that is not attached by emotional obsession to a male protector. A rare woman, indeed. She is like the actress Vashti in *Villette*, who seems to burst into flames before lonely Lucy's eyes, publicly setting herself afire with her female creativity. 'It is a woman's vision', says critic Jane Miller in her study, *Women Writing about Men* 'and a vision of a woman, the most astonishing experience of Lucy's life for being a vision of female power unmediated by men and beyond their judgment and understanding' (Miller, 1986:96).

Bertha is conspicuously detached from the conventions of romance, a gigantic, obscene joke of a bride, a laughing hyena lurking around the subtle parlour games of attraction and seduction and revelation that count for everything in selecting and securing a mate. 'That is *my wife*', Rochester says to introduce Jane to Bertha, having just wrestled with the cursing Bertha and tied her to a chair. He hopes that Jane won't need to have the joke of marriage explained when she literally sees the punchline. 'Such is the sole conjugal embrace I am ever to know – such are the endearments which are to solace my leisure hours!' (*296*).

But Bertha is not only a feminist comedienne. In Jane's experience at Thornfield, she acts as a powerful threat to the assumption that women are fulfilled only in marriage, and she haunts Jane as a possibility, an alternative to marrying Rochester, and finally an obstacle to their growing love and marriage. Three battles are fought before she is defeated definitively in death.

COURTSHIP PART ONE: TAMING FEMALE DESIRE

Bertha's first wild night engulfs Rochester in flames in his own bed. She literally creeps downstairs, sets fire to the curtains on Rochester's bed, probably accidentally, laughs in Jane's ear and leaves a candle outside her locked door, then disappears without having been seen. What provokes Bertha and what does she mean?

Jane spends an evening reflecting on her growing intimacy with Rochester, and its inherent dangers. She struggles over old conflicts between solitude and dependence, and between identifying with men rather than with women. What woman has resolved these to her satisfaction, especially in adolescence, when choices seem absolute and irreversible, feminism and femininity seem to demand opposing resolutions? The attractions of Rochester's greater knowledge and experience charge Jane's sense of him:

> I had a keen delight in receiving the new ideas he offered, in imagining the new pictures he portrayed, or followed him in thought through the new regions he disclosed. . . . The ease of his manner freed me from painful restraint; the friendly frankness as correct as cordial, with which he treated me, drew me to him.
> (*149*)

What worries her is her increasing dependence on Rochester, which develops nearly to the point of merging her sense of self with him, 'as if he were my relation'; he becomes for Jane what Adrienne Rich calls 'the phantom of the man-who-would-understand, the lost brother, the twin' (Rich, 1984: 258).

Fulfilment through a man is the test of 'true love and perfect union': does he meet my every need, fill my every thought, answer my every question? Jane thinks it looks promising: 'my thin crescent-destiny seemed to enlarge; the blanks of existence were filled up; my bodily health improved; I gathered flesh and strength' (*149*). Such a self-description appears to fulfil the promise of romance, yet why does it evoke Bertha's qualities – the moon, the flesh, and unfeminine strength? What calls forth Bertha from the attic that night, to look on Rochester in his bed? Jane's restlessness that night: 'I hardly know whether I had slept or not after this musing ' (*150*) – her burning candle, her revery's uncensored passion, and her access to Rochester's bed and body all implicate her in Bertha's crime of setting the fire. Bertha gets intimate: she laughs her demonic laugh 'at the very key-hole of my chamber door' so 'I thought at first the goblin-laughter stood by my bedside – or rather, crouched by my pillow' (*151*) – lurking, taunting Jane with strange familiarity.

In wanting to believe that Rochester is the answer, Jane must suppress any doubts that he can fulfil her hungry quest. She has quite a shopping list, and Charlotte Brontë gives her quite a loaded hero. (As a certain romance writer said recently, 'When you get to make up your own hero, he can be *really good*.') Bertha has *her* doubts, however, so she comes out as Jane sleeps, to provide her commentary on the affair. As always, first is 'a demoniac laugh – low, suppressed, and deep' (*151*). Then Bertha's creeping climaxes in tongues of flame darting around the sleeping Rochester.

Bertha is that hungry angry solitary woman vengefully haunting the two lovers who dream of their escape into the world of romantic love. She destroys this dream world with her fire. 'A dream had scarcely approached my ear', Jane says, 'when it fled affrighted, scared by a marrow-freezing incident enough' (*151*). Nightmare, ghost, Bertha uncannily flares into fiery reality, momentarily banishing Jane's love affair to the land of lost dreams.

Resourceful Jane snuffs Bertha's threat and saves Rochester – which increases their intimacy and his debt to her, all to be repaid in time by a security bond of marriage. What exactly is the threat, this fire that Jane douses? 'Passion!' my students all shout, sure of the meaning of that symbol every time. Bertha as a demanding female desire threatens to annihilate the romantic scenario of Rochester as protector and provider of Jane's social identity. Female passion has no place in Victorian marriage, as

Bertha relentlessly reminds us. The marriage itself is the satisfaction of desire to the bride, who is forever fulfilled by the social security she has won, and the maternity sure to follow. Jane, here, struggles to internalize this paradox of womanhood, that *femininity is dependent on male desire but is threatened by female desire*. In restless revery Jane calls forth a vision of this paradox, is thrilled then alarmed by its potential to devour, and dispels it with a cold shower.

Bertha's second attack is also against a male protector – her brother who helped arrange her marriage and who accedes to her imprisonment in Rochester's attic. Richard Mason arrives when Rochester, dressed as a pipe-smoking old gypsy woman, is craftily trying to trick secrets out of the house party's single ladies. The effeminate gentleman, Mason, is as far from masculinity – lacking power, firmness, thought, and command – as the gypsy is from femininity. Jane's confusion is compounded when Rochester throws off his disguise only to reveal a mysterious and threatening link to Mason. When Mason sneaks up to see his sister that night, he gets bitten for his trouble. Rochester covers up by explaining to his guests that the noise was a servant's bad dream (Grace Pool takes the fall again), then takes Jane to the third story to nurse the bleeding man, asking her not to speak while he gets a doctor. She does, trying to ignore the snarling in the very next room, 'terminating in Grace Poole's own goblin ha! ha! *She* then was there.' When Rochester returns at dawn with the doctor, Mason revives and speaks. 'She bit me', he whines. 'She worried me like a tigress, when Rochester got the knife from her.' Knife? Teeth? Tigress? Worse yet: 'she sucked the blood: she said she'd drain my heart' (*214*), he claims. Is this woman really a vampire?

Bertha's second attack mimics her first. Again Jane mops up the blood Bertha spills, and thus again secures intimacy as Rochester's helpmeet because she shows she can be trusted to keep the (dirty) secret (of female desire). Again the attack occurs just after Jane and Rochester have become more intimate (the gypsy scene). Again the intimacy comes through Jane being known by Rochester when he reads her character, which causes her to feel him as herself: the gypsy was 'familiar to me as my own face in a glass – as the speech of my own tongue' (*203*). Again the tension is over this merging – loss – of self, again Jane asks, 'Where was I? Did I wake or sleep? Had I been dreaming? Did I dream still?' And again, that night, Bertha strikes out for Jane.

Yet this time, Jane gets closer to Bertha, as she realizes when she listens to her laugh and finds that she cannot stop the flow of blood from the wound the woman has made:

> Here then I was in the third story, fastened into one of its mystic cells; night around me; a pale and bloody spectacle under my eyes and hands; a murderess hardly separated from me by a single door: yes – that was appalling – the rest I could bear; but I shuddered at the thought of Grace Poole bursting out upon me. (*211–12*)

In describing how psychic self-policing works and feels, Jane Eyre is as clear as daylight and as spooky as nightmares. Envisioning the bloody spectacle wreaked by our own feared monstrosity, we shudder and fasten oursleves into a safe cell of innocence, ask no questions, and wait for dawn, Rochester, and the doctor. 'I was afraid of some one coming out of the inner room', Jane later tells Rochester, who replies masterfully, 'But I had fastened the door – I had the key in my pocket' (*218*).

All night Jane hears Bertha, 'the wild beast or the fiend in yonder side den', and thinks worrisome thoughts:

> What crime was this, that lived incarnate in this sequestered mansion, and could neither be expelled nor subdued by the owner? – What mystery, that broke out, now in fire and now in blood, at the deadest hours of night? What creature was it, that, masked in an ordinary woman's face and shape, uttered the voice, now of a mocking demon, and anon of a carrion-seeking bird of prey? (*212*)

Here Bertha is featured as the central mystery of this gothic plot, coloured in with all the key gothic crayons (and power from nature) of demon, fire, blood, nightmare, masked female, and vampire bat. Intriguingly, she is called a 'crime incarnate' that 'could neither be expelled nor subdued by the owner'. This can be read in two ways – a teasing tension 'hardly separated by a single door', according to my reading of Bertha.

A feminist reading asserts that female desire can neither be expelled nor subdued, neither ignored nor controlled by the owner husband, so his crime against nature (female desire is natural) is to incarcerate her as the criminal: she becomes *his* crime incarnate. This has become a radical feminist, dark vision of patriarchal, heterosexual oppression: female sexuality is criminalized and caged by jailer-males.

The second reading, conventionally feminine, is that female desire is itself the crime incarnate – a living enactment of illegitimate, unnatural feeling that (in Jane's case) can neither be expelled nor subdued by its owner, the woman herself, whether by will, reason, or denial. The woman must internalize a Grace Poole for her Bertha, because she, not her husband, is responsible for keeping her own house in order.

Jane wavers between these two readings of female desire while at Thornfield, haunted by the question: 'Is her desire criminal?' She plays it both ways, in feminine fashion giving Rochester his daytime mastery of her, and in feminist fashion giving Bertha her night walks of vengeance. This is the delicious tension of the novel for me as a female reader: can Jane perhaps have both? The Bertha paradox at this moment is about Jane's desire to have Rochester *and*, not or, a bed afflare with tongues of flame. If love is union, mutuality, mirroring (Jane's hazy romantic feelings), then why cannot passion be one of the reflections, shared mutually? How far can Jane's bid for fully equal partnership be tolerated? Whose crime is Bertha – the husband for imprisoning her, perhaps initiating her vengeful fury? or the wife for having a nature deemed unnatural? *Is* it unnatural?

Women are promised both love and passion by romantic fiction, which seems to solve several paradoxes of sexual relations that real life does not. First, it turns out that the hero is not indifferent or repulsed or otherwise engaged, but aflame with a desire as intense as the heroine has kept locked in her secret self. This mutual attraction, invariably described as a mirror-moment of self-recognition, magically dissolves all

those impenetrably dense and inextricable gender differences –
into air, or, for the inquisitive, into the denouement dustbin of
illusions dispelled, misunderstandings cleared up, and disguises shed. True love means perfect union, so the civil war
between the sexes is suddenly over, and revisionist history
reworks the carnage into cute courtship stories. Romance
promises passionate fulfilment at this moment – but never
quite delivers it.

The climactic point of revelation, that the hero *loves* her,
provides the opening and security clearance for the heroine's
revelation: she's *hot* for him too. While apparently a moment of
mutuality and mirroring, actually, the sexes exchange complementary and not identical tokens of esteem. He professes
love: he *needs* her. That is the deep, dark, unmanly secret he
entrusts to her. He needs her emotionally, and domestically,
and morally, and socially, and reproductively to serve him. Of
course no-one but a feminist would make him admit that,
especially to himself. He'll give her in exchange, loyalty, social
security, marriage. On the other hand, when she professes love,
she admits she *wants* him. That's the unfeminine secret she
entrusts to him. Her sexuality, dangerously illegitimate if
undirected to a man and untied to love, and therefore
unspeakable, is miraculously born at this moment of safe
arrival in a man's arms, apparently created out of his need for
her, and certainly forever afterwards dependent on him. Her
desire is only admissible as love – requited love. Otherwise it
will destroy her – witness Bertha. Jane warns herself of this very
thing when she first realizes she's falling in love with Rochester:

> It does good to no woman to be flattered by her superior, who
> cannot possibly intend to marry her; and it is madness in all
> women to let a secret love kindle within them, which, if
> unreturned and unknown, must devour the life that feeds it; and,
> if discovered and responded to, must lead, *ignis-fatuus*-like, into
> miry wilds whence there is no extrication.
>
> Listen, then, Jane Eyre, to your sentence: to-morrow, place the
> glass before you, and draw in chalk your own picture, faithfully;
> without softening one defect: omit no harsh line, smooth away
> no displeasing irregularity; write under it, 'Portrait of a
> Governess, disconnected, poor, and plain.' (*163*)

She warns all women of the danger of female desire, in highly incendiary terms: it is madness, it is self-devouring, it will lead you into a lethal quagmire – all Bertha's problems. Control yourself by creating a picture of yourself as a veritable Grace Poole, and inscribe it 'governess', 'orphan', 'single woman', 'ugly woman': 'unmarriageable'. 'Governess' means self-government.

The morning after Bertha's second attack, Jane is called away to Gateshead from her midnight pitch of desire and the promise of having it all. It's the three Reed women who douse her passion this time – three female Fates: the bitter widow, the bitter nun, the bitter society marriage. Jane reads them as warnings of the self-destroying frustrations endured by women unfulfilled by a man's true love. This sobering visit, during which Jane literally serves each woman's neurotic needs for a week, is enough to 'lower her wick' and compel her to rethink her Berthaesque demands of Rochester as a husband. On her return, '"Pass, Janet," said he, making room for me to cross the stile.... All I had now to do was to obey him in silence: no need for me to colloquise further' (*248*). Her impulse to speak overcomes her, but she doesn't sound like the Jane who used to speak up to Rochester: '"Thank you, Mr. Rochester, for your great kindness. I am strangely glad to get back again to you; and wherever you are is my home – my only home"' (*248*). Here, we have a silent and submissive Jane re-entering Rochester's domain, so glad to escape Gateshead's past and future threats of female solitude that she grovels in gratitude.

Bertha's third attack occurs the night before Jane and Rochester's wedding, a face-to-face-in-the-mirror confrontation. The two women are separated now only by a glass. Bertha tries on Jane's veil in the mirror and then tears it in two and tramples on it; she sees Jane and snuffs her candle in her face, and – Jane faints. 'Now sir, tell me who and what that woman was?' (*286*), Jane demands of Rochester the next morning when he returns home. Rochester tells her she was dreaming. Jane counters that she found the actual ripped veil. Rochester amends his story without losing his patronizing manner. (Why do I hear Spencer Tracey here, talking to

Katherine Hepburn?): 'Now, Janet, I'll explain to you all about it. It was half dream, half reality' (*287*) — it was Grace Poole, house mystery to be explained at some future date at Rochester's convenience 'Are you satisfied Jane? Do you accept my solution of the mystery?' (*287*). Jane, always obliging to the point of wifeliness after one of Bertha's hostile outbreaks, thinks, 'Satisfied I was not, but to please him I endeavoured to appear so – relieved, I certainly did feel; so I answered him with a contented smile' (*287*). Rochester suggests that Jane retreat to the nursery, where 'there is room enough in Adèle's little bed for you. . . . And fasten the door securely on the inside' (*288*). Back in the nun's mystic cell, then, where it's safe from Big B.

That night Jane does not sleep at all: 'With little Adèle in my arms, I watched the slumber of childhood – so tranquil, so passionless, so innocent. . . . She seemed the emblem of my past life; and he, I was now to array myself to meet, the dread, but adored, type of my unknown future day' (*288*). End of chapter, needless to say.

Bertha represents Jane's sexual fears on the eve of her sexual initiation, that much is clear. And the infant that Jane dreams is in her care as Rochester strides manfully off into his broader horizon – reminds us that female sexuality almost inevitably included maternity and irreversible retreat into the female sphere. Jane has much more to lose than her virginity. What will become of the educated woman whose independent, cultivated mind wooed and won Rochester? When she imagines her next step, from passionless innocent girl (Adèle), she sees a 'dread, but adored' *he* who set the type, so to speak, of her future self. Wifehood, her 'unknown future day', is defined by the man she will 'array [herself] to meet', fashion herself to match. The female pronoun literally disappears into the unknown of marriage, where the generic 'he' sets the future type. The married woman is by law *femme couverte*, perhaps suffocated under the title or the body of her husband.

Now it is becoming clear what the terms of marriage to Rochester will be for Jane. His version insists rather pornographically on Jane the scolding nun, his 'girl-bride' (*260*) innocent who can redeem the sinning man from his mid-life crisis. His version writes out Bertha as a figment of Jane's imagination, and insists on Grace Poole as the 'real' and mundane explanation for Jane's three wild nights. And he asks Jane, in a kind of marriage proposal, to accept his 'solution of the mystery' of female desire: it's a dream, not a reality; and to accept his 'type' of marriage: Bertha erased. Jane is not satisfied with it, to her feminist credit, but 'endeavoured to appear so', practising a good wifely faked 'content', so relieved is she to recast the voracious face of Bertha from a woman, a bride, to nothing but a bad dream (*287*).

When, for the third time, Jane balks in fearful anticipation of what she has to lose in marriage, Bertha comes down that night to scorn the veil's coverage of the bride, mocking the thin pretence of purity and innocence with a loud ri-i-i-p and red-hot tap dance, just like Snow White's bitchy stepmother. She makes Jane look again in her mirror at her own innocence and sexual expectations. What she sees is Bertha's 'savage face' of rapacious intensity, engorged with sexual excitement: inflamed and dark and purple and bloodshot. When desire rears its head, take a look in the mirror, lady: it's *ugly*, it's 'the foul German spectre – the Vampyre' (*286*) – a blood-sucking, man-eating monster. Eeek! The lady faints in horror and banishes her closest friend and worst enemy. Bertha's role is again to threaten the terms of romance and marriage for Jane, mocking bridal purity and innocence as some lunatic joke – which Jane's innocence can't let her understand, but which her night-vision sees and remembers.

Victorian images of animalistic desire provide books full of matter for feminist inquiry. The image that haunts me is Virginia Woolf's memory, in *Moments of Being*, of looking into the mirror as a girl and envisioning an animal peering over her shoulder, grotesque and leering. Was it connected to her memory of her half-brother's abuse of her, she later wonders. 'I cannot be sure. But I have always remembered the other face in the glass, whether it was a dream or a fact, and that it frightened me' (Woolf, 1978:69).

Feminists may explain and explain again, but for Jane the trembling bride, for *all* women taking a close look in the matrimonial mirror, fingering the veil and wondering whether the dress is a 'gown, sheet, or shroud' (285), the question must be answered now, and not just theoretically, either, but practically, if possible. Is Bertha a dream or a fact? We post-Freudians can smugly predict the return of the repressed, and gothic novel readers can too. The answer, Bertha, has gone back upstairs for the night, leaving Jane sleepless and doubtful about whether Rochester's solution, namely Grace Poole, can really cover all there is to know about the hot and bloody nights at Thornfield Hall.

Next day, at the wedding, Jane gets her answer when Bertha's name definitively interrupts the union-in-the-making. A solicitor stands up and presents 'an insuperable impediment, a wife now living' (292) madly in Rochester's attic. At last the poor woman is socially recognized! In a brilliant flash of the uncanny, Bertha becomes Rochester's wife in Jane's place. Bertha the ghost, the laugh, the nightmare, and the figment of Jane's imagination flares into full reality and legitimacy because she is Rochester's wife. And Jane, poor Jane, vanishes into a mere shadow of her former self. Almost a bride, blushing in full flesh and blood, she is suddenly cast onto the cold hillside, alone and palely loitering: 'Jane Eyre, who had been an ardent, expectant woman – almost a bride – was a cold, solitary girl again: her life was pale, her prospects were desolate' (298).

What bursts Jane's bubble of romance? What, quite literally, prevents her from becoming a passionless Victorian wife? We have our answer now: Bertha. As Jane's 'still living' female desire, Bertha could neither be expelled nor subdued by the owner. Oh the frustration! Here was Jane finally willing to make the marriage deal, all doubts suppressed, Rochester's version agreed to – then: Bertha's back! Can't tame her, divorce her, reason with her, kill her – she just is.

This is an unambiguously feminist moment in the novel, this meeting between Jane and the unbudgable Bertha. First, Bertha cannot be denied, she is 'the living proof' (297): she is a real, strong, and passionate woman, not Thornfield's ghost, Jane's fiction, or Rochester's lie. And she confirms the reality of all of

Jane's (feminist) doubts, not only about Rochester as rake and tyrant, but also about the wish for ethereal (bodiless) romance between elf and Gytrash, which Jane had winsomely harbored since meeting her prince-on-a-charger that moonlit night.

Now literally out of the closet, legally recognized, and seen by all in full-colour flesh and blood, Bertha is centre stage with her monstrous feminist joke about marriage and womanhood. But only she gets the joke; as the unconscious Other, Bertha always laughs alone. She paradoxically demands recognition (aflame symbolically, metaphorically dripping with blood) but eludes articulation. Female sexuality, like Bertha's overlarge and overactive body, is the unspeaking and unspeakable problem.

Seeing Bertha is the final and fairly fatal encounter between Jane and her version of female sexuality. First she heard it in Bertha's laugh, then she saw its effects on men (Rochester afire in bed, Mason's bloody cheek and gouged arm), then she saw it through a dream and mirror (vampyre face of passion), finally, she meets it directly in its unmediated being.

She moves through frames as levels of consciousness, suggesting a peeling away of layers of socialized repression. *Jane Eyre* resembles the more complicated narrative form of *Wuthering Heights* (written a year earlier) in this opening of boxes-within-boxes by the narrator. The reader follows Lockwood into the world of *Wuthering Heights*, hearing increasingly intimate stories that culminate in the romantic point of passionate union. Catherine's 'I AM Heathcliffe!' is the mirror-moment of female fulfilment of the romantic quest. Imaginatively (only) Catherine can appropriate Heathcliffe's Byronic adventurism. But *Wuthering Heights*, unlike *Jane Eyre*, doesn't believe in the successful domestication of passion between equals. Catherine dies – self-destructs! – with the realization that she and Heathcliffe are united in feeling but divided in social possibility, real life's pragmatic and conscientious commentary that places passion with*in* reason. Catherine deliriously retreats into her bedroom mirror's world. Jane Eyre, Catherine's eminently practical older sister, doesn't die in a fit of pique, but does necessarily choose a path of self-denial. Just as brave as Catherine in calling forth her most deeply feared desires, Jane

Eyre takes a look in *her* matrimonial mirror and sees, as Catherine does, a nightmare version of herself. Jane's is a conventional Victorian nightmare of female sexuality, a worst-case scenario of all systems gone haywire: Bertha has regressed to animalism – vicious, inarticulate, and mad – both genetically through her mother ('Her mother, the Creole, was both a mad woman and a drunkard!' (*294*)), and degeneratively through her 'excesses' (she's 'intemperate and unchaste' (*309*)), which had 'prematurely developed the germs of insanity' (*309*). Nature and nurture, both irreversibly corrupted femininities.

If Bertha's noises, hints, jokes, and warnings haven't been enough to frighten Jane about the destructive capability of female passion, she now has two utterly literal ways in which to understand Bertha's warning for her self and life. One is her own sight of Bertha – both women unspeaking. The other is Bertha's story – but told by Rochester – again, both women unspeaking.

Jane's encounter is visual, entirely sensual, a picture without a caption. She herself sees Bertha as *she* is. This way of seeing evokes Charlotte Brontë's description (in a letter to George Henry Lewes) of imagination as a powerful female authority for creativity, fiction-making:

> Imagination is a strong, restless faculty. When she shows us bright pictures, are we never to look at them, and try to reproduce them? And when she is eloquent, and speaks rapidly and urgently in our ear, are we not to write to her dictation?
>
> (Peters, 1986: 207)

Strong and restless and compelling, 'she' has something she's trying to tell us. Is it translatable? Understandable? Desirable? Desire itself?

First Jane sees an 'it':

> What it was, whether beast or human being, one could not, at first sight, tell: it grovelled, seemingly, on all fours; it snatched and growled like some strange wild animal: but it was covered with clothing; and a quantity of dark, grizzled hair, wild as a mane, hid its head and face. (*295*)

Then the face: 'she parted her shaggy locks from her visage, and gazed wildly at her visions. I recognised well that purple face – those bloated features' (*295*). It is a she, a remembered vision in Jane's midnight mirror.

Then the act:

> Mr. Rochester flung me behind him: the lunatic sprang and grappled his throat viciously, and laid her teeth to his cheek: they struggled. She was a big woman, in stature almost equalling her husband, and corpulent besides: she showed virile force in the contest – more than once she almost throttled him, athletic as he was. He could have settled her with a well-planted blow; but he would not strike: he would only wrestle. At last he mastered her arms; Grace Poole gave him a cord. (*296*)

The irrationality and physicality, the animalistically violent struggle of husand and wife, suggests Freud's child's-eye view of the primal scene, but from a more particular angle, that of the pubescent female. It is a triangle, with Jane the innocent child protected by strong-but-kind Rochester, enduring the un-provoked attack of his oversized wife in all her unnatural 'virile force'. *Female passion is literally attacking male protectorship of female purity.* This is what Bertha's first three attacks had so broadly hinted. The primal scene revised from a feminist perspective reveals each time the paradox of femininity: that *femininity is dependent on male desire and loyalty but threatened by female desire.* Female purity is the condition of male love and loyalty, and in turn, male love and loyalty are the secure signs of successful femininity. Rochester's treatment of the intrusive and inversive Bertha only serves to show how dire the consequences are for the unfeminine 'it'.

> 'That is *my wife*,' said he . . . 'And this is what I wished to have,' (laying his hand on my shoulder): 'this young girl, who stands so grave and quiet at the mouth of hell, looking collectedly at the gambols of a demon. I wanted her just as a change after that fierce ragout. Wood and Briggs, look at the difference! Compare these clear eyes and the red balls yonder – this face with that mask – this form with that bulk, then judge me, priest of the gospel and man of the law . . .' (*296*)

Who wouldn't prefer girlhood to such a nightmare of sexuality, especially as a condition of love? To be grave, quiet, and collected – to control rather than unleash passion – is the route to Rochester's heart, wifehood, and social security, Jane learns. Readers of *Jane Eyre*, often female adolescents themselves, may well ask whether female desire is still so dangerous, illegitimate, and repulsive. And whether saving rather than spending desire is the route out of the prison of adolescence into womanhood.

Jane's interpretation and loyalty is on the side of the kind husband who would not strike but only wrestle and tie his wife, using the constraint provided by his handy little policewoman-servant. Bertha's role here is as monitory as it gets, causing Jane's most regressive reaction yet: back to girlhood. Like Bertha's other attacks, it is 'a marrow-freezing incident enough' to shrink-wrap Jane's 'ardent, expectant womanhood' back into 'a cold, solitary girl again' (*298*). The all-too-literal sight of an active female sexuality catapults Jane back in horror from the threshold of sexual experience, and definitively dampens her desires. Jane again throws cold water over Bertha's 'inflamed visage' of feminist rebellion, and this time snuffs Bertha's imaginative power over Jane.

Jane's finally seeing what had been haunting her, dispels all Bertha's power as an unconscious symbol. Bertha is simply too far out for Jane ever to identify with consciously. All the force of the uncanny, of Jane's secret identification with Bertha, is destroyed when the wildest of beings is seen to be less, not more, than human, physically powerful but without self-control, a being more 'it' than 'she'. And, perhaps more important, a being despised and hated *in Rochester's eyes*. Whatever force Bertha is to have in Jane's life can no longer be in her imaginative unconscious, where the sights and sounds are gothic and *uncaptioned by social reality*. Henceforward, Bertha's meaning cannot be closeted in Jane's wild nights of fantasy, but is 'out' in the daylight world, where her behaviour and motives and nature are all a matter for moral judgment. No wonder Jane drops her like a hot potato! Too dangerous. Jane can afford only pity for – what to call her? 'That unfortunate lady' (*303*) hardly captures Bertha's essence or social unsuitability. And this is the heart of Jane's problem with Bertha: her meaning for Jane remains unspeakable; Jane and Bertha remain unspeaking to each other. Bertha is felt and seen by Jane and by women readers of the novel, but her meaning for women is never articulated. It is untranslatable into the social world, where there are no positive terms for wild women, loose women, sexual women. That is why Jane sees and feels Bertha as a being of gothic fiction, but has no words to translate her into the realism of her social relations with Rochester. *Jane loses Bertha's power* as unconscious, female sexual symbol *because she cannot speak her*, to Rochester, or to herself.

So near, dear reader, and yet so far. Ghost, but hauntingly recognizable, Bertha remains there for us as a possibility of female desire unattached to male desire. She exists in fiction as a kind of wild promise yet to be realized, yet to be translated into social reality. Like Charlotte Brontë's description of imagination as a female-to-female form of inspired communication and empowerment, Bertha represents power from the other world, where fiction and female desire have free play, and where readers of fiction go to be fed. Bertha gives rise to the radical question: Is it fiction which best feeds female desire? Rochester as fiction or Heathcliffe as fiction, are insistently female creations, not pale imitations of paler, real-life men.

When Bertha is transferred from the secret dream-world of female possibility to the real, social world as Rochester's wife, her power as female Other is easily contained, inverted, and dispelled by *words*. Rochester, as master of social meanings, freely labels Bertha with all the contemptible labels applicable to deviant women. His narration of her story interprets her as wicked from the get-go. What can Jane reply? What alternative – positive or even neutral – version of female passion and sexuality, much less rebellion and revenge, is there? An entire alternative moral system might be imagined by Jane (her life's work, and ours as feminists), but it has yet no social reality, no words. As when Brocklehurst had asked her if she was a good girl, Jane finds it 'Impossible to reply to this in the affirmative: my little world held a contrary opinion: I was silent' (*34*).

Struck into silence by male control of the terms of moral censure, Jane listens to Rochester's gripping tale of betrayal by the seductress, Bertha. Only *this time* she will fashion a reply to the man himself, and will - true triumph! - persuade him of the validity of her version of female-male moral relations.

After the primal scene, her last tangle with Bertha, Jane locks herself into her room to exert her overwhelmingly rigorous self-control: 'And now I thought: till now I had only heard, seen, moved - followed up and down where I was led or dragged - watched event rush on event, disclosure open beyond disclosure; but *now, I thought*' (297).

> Jane Eyre, who had been an ardant, expectant woman - almost a bride - was a cold, solitary girl again: her life was pale, her prospects were desolate. A Christmas frost had come at midsummer; a white December storm had whirled over June; ice glazed the ripe apples, drifts crushed the blowing roses; ... My hopes were all dead - struck with a subtle doom. ... I looked on my cherished wishes, yesterday so blooming and glowing; they lay stark, chill, livid corpses, that could never revive. (298)

In the interior landscape she conjures, romance is cast as summer, reality as a killing winter. Certainly, her circumstances warrant such a picture, but Jane is not content to be held by circumstance. She takes the leash into her own hands to render self-punishment, making over harsh reality with her own harsher reason, and blighted romance into her own corrupted sickly feelings. The heavy tread of thought on the prance of feelings is crushing indeed. Her thoughts themselves frost the apples of desire, her reason crushes the roses of blooming feeling, her conscience blights the purity of her love.

We are back in the cell of the mystic nun, undergoing the rigours of applied conscience to the illicit pleasures of summery feeling. Never has the hope of emotional fulfilment been so great, never has the necessity to check it been so harshly summoned. With grim pride she announces the result of her struggle: 'Conscience, turned tyrant, held passion by the throat' (299). Throttling desire is one way of finishing off Bertha, and between the killing frost of conscience and reining to the point of choking with reason, she manages to govern herself well enough to turn to the project of governing Rochester.

COURTSHIP PART TWO: TAMING MALE DEMAND

What has become of Jane's love for Rochester? It, too, has been frosted by the winter and rough weather. 'It shivered in my heart, like a suffering child in a cold cradle' (*298*). Now interestingly, Jane 'would not ascribe vice to him' who has presumably given their love-child its 'sickness and anguish' (*298*). Instead, she quite irrationally but all too femininely attributes the problem to impetuous male desire, the solution to which is female flight.

> Mr. Rochester was not to me what he had been; for he was not what I had thought him. I would not ascribe vice to him; I would not say he had betrayed me: but the attribute of stainless truth was gone from his idea; and from his presence I must go: *that* I perceived well. When–how–wither, I could not yet discern: but he himself, I doubted not, would hurry me from Thornfield. Real affection, it seemed, he could not have for me; it had been only fitful passion, that was balked; he would want me no more. I should fear even to cross his path now: my view must be hateful to him. Oh, how blind had been my eyes! How weak my conduct! (*298*)

Jane has worked her way, in the course of this meditation, stealthily back towards romance. From a blind fate acting as 'Old Man Winter' on her fair chances, she comes to blame her own blindness as the problem. If she hadn't put on the rose-coloured spectacles of romance, she would never have fallen to a fallen man's deluded love song. Jane's conscience lights only on herself here; it does not prosecute Rochester.

The real question, it appears, is not what has become of Jane's love (it's only sick, not dead), but what has become of Jane's identity as a loved woman? Her feelings are in the end left in Rochester's hands, because the love-child is her 'master's – which he had created' (*298*). Its fate seems to be in his hands.

So she comes to hang herself on that tattered old question: Does he still love me?

He does, dear reader, he does. When Jane emerges from her room, he's waiting to tell her all – his unchanged feelings and remorse. 'Will you ever forgive me?' (*300*). How many times in the history of western civilization has an abusive male resecured, even tightened, the loyalty of his wife or lover with this plea? It is a warped, sadistic turn on the classic male–female exchange: confession of male need elicits female moral service, to the point of self-sacrifice. Jane's response:

> Reader! – I forgave him at the moment, and on the spot. There was such deep remorse in his eyes, such true pity in his tone, such manly energy in his manner; *and besides, there was such unchanged love in his whole look and mien – I forgave him all:* yet not in words, not outwardly; only at my heart's core. (300–1; my emphasis)

From this bottomless pit of feminine self-sacrifice, Jane cannily protects herself by not telling Rochester that her feelings are entirely dependent on his. Jane confesses only to her readers her secret female vulnerability. Witholding is her only power over Rochester now. Jane's colossal power to contain, direct, and manage whole armies on the field of emotional terrain is given opportunity in the ensuing battle with Rochester over control of the terms of their relationship. Will the master or the governess prove the better general? The man has virility but the woman has purity; male and female virtues compete for domination.

Having assured herself of Rochester's unchanged love, there's one little matter Jane would like to clear up: Bertha, the meaning of Bertha. As becomes clear, she's hardly solvable; Bertha remains the tough question at the centre of female-male moral relations.

Rochester begins, again and again, with a kind of sweaty relish, to absolve himself by denouncing Bertha. His explanation of his motives rests on the fact that Bertha is a witch.

'that demon's vicinage is poisoned, and always was. But I'll shut up Thornfield Hall: I'll nail up the front door, and board the lower windows; I'll give Mrs Poole two hundred a year to live here with *my wife*, as you term that fearful hag: Grace will do much for money, and she shall have her son, the keeper of Grimsby Retreat, to bear her company and be at hand to give her aid, in the paroxysms, when *my wife* is prompted by her familiar to burn people in their beds at night, to stab them, to bite their flesh from their bones, and so on –'

'Sir,' I interrupted him, 'you are inexorable for that unfortunate lady: you speak of her with hate – with vindictive antipathy. It is cruel – she cannot help being mad.'

'Jane, my little darling (so I will call you, for so you are), you don't know what you are talking about; you misjudge me again: it is not because she is mad I hate her. If you were mad, do you think I should hate you?'

'I do indeed, sir.'

'Then you are mistaken, and you know nothing about me, and nothing about the sort of love of which I am capable.' (*303*)

Jane interrupts this self-interested male rant with her most pointed feminist point, her one and only defence of Bertha. But what quickly undermines Jane's position, making it a very solitary and transient point, is her need for love.

Jane's worst fear is that Rochester hates the unalloyed essence of wild womanhood, Bertha's reckless autonomy, and like many men considers it witchiness (now called bitchiness), so his love is conditional on Jane's keeping herself in check. Rochester's denial that he hates Bertha for her madness is hardly supported by the abundance of evidence to the contrary, as Jane notes. By turning the question to his infinite love for Jane, even if mad, in contrast to his repulsion from Bertha, Rochester underlines that his love for her depends on her difference from Bertha. If Jane were mad, he coos, his love would gently bind her, his arms would be her fond and restrictive straitjacket, he would be her only watcher and nurse. Is this really a consolation, or is it a subtle confirmation that Rochester's love draws the boundaries around Jane's appropriate conduct? He alone defines her as a beloved woman, and within his conception of womanhood there is room for plain Jane, but none of – nothing of – Bertha.

Bertha is the term for 'not-womanhood', unsuccessful, untrue femininity, unrespected and unloved by Rochester, who defines the unrespectable and unlovable. Bertha proves hard to budge in Jane and Rochester's moral discourse about marital behaviour and responsibility for men and women. Rochester uses Bertha to support the double standard, to justify his rakish conduct, and to characterize his love of Jane.

Yet, in the course of their climactic and definitive confrontation, Jane heroically finds a way to dispense with Bertha in defining her own womanhood, by using moral terms largely divorced from Rochester's double standard terms of male/female, virgin/whore, wife/mistress. This is Jane's feminist triumph, as will be seen, but it has a high price. *To refuse Bertha as a moral term is to abandon Bertha as a moral possibility*, as the symbol of an active and positive, autonomous female desire. The unbudgable fact is that Bertha has only negative value in the marriage market. As a coin of exchange, female purity is gold, while female desire is more like debt, all too vulnerable to rakish debt-buyers. Jane finds a way to set her own brideprice with complete moral integrity and autonomy – a small step for one woman, a giant leap for womankind. But she cannot change the marriage market itself, or the desirability – virtual necessity – of marriage for women in a society that punishes single women with the lives of 'nuns – with their close cell, their iron lamp, their robe strait as a shroud, their bed narrow as a coffin' (Brontë, 1974:376).

We reach the limits of *Jane Eyre's* feminism at this point, and it is the limit of most women's feminism, particularly married, middle-class women, for very good reasons. Making her own best deal in marriage is an attainable goal for each woman working alone. Anything further looks barely possible, or even desirable, if fulfilment in marriage is to be protected. Charlotte Brontë looked further than Jane Eyre's case, and saw a million more – saw how systematically women come to 'choose' to make their way through marriage. Nowhere more poignantly is Charlotte Brontë's feminism better described, than in her first letter to Elizabeth Gaskell, 17 August 1850. She refers to the 'Westminster Review':

in which there was an article entitled 'Woman's Mission' (the phrase is hackneyed), containing a great deal that seemed to me just and sensible. Men begin to regard the position of woman in another light than they used to do; and a few men, whose sympathies are fine and whose sense of justice is strong, think and speak of it with a candour that commands my admiration. They say, however – and, to an extent, truly – that the amelioration of our condition depends on ourselves. Certainly there are evils which our own efforts will best reach; but as certainly there are other evils – deep-rooted in the foundations of the social system – which no efforts of ours can touch; of which we cannot complain; of which it is advisable not too often to think.

(Gaskell, 1975:421–2)

Individual marital terms are negotiable, Jane is bent on proving that terrain is 'a field for women's efforts, and exercise for their faculties' that will at least win them a more expansive future lot as wives wielding some degree of domestic power. The moral regeneration – even subordination – of the fallen male is, for Jane and most women, the most obvious 'evil which our own efforts will best reach' (Gaskell, 1975:421–2). The rest, deep-rooted in the foundations of the social system, may be seen in the different female fates minutely examined in all Charlotte Brontë's novels, the 'lots' circumscribed by the strictly drawn lines between single and married women, governesses and ladies, and pure and lost women. Harriet Martineau realized this feminist power in writing: 'I want to be doing something with the pen, since no other means of action in politics are in a woman's power' (Hall, 1985: 15).

Jane's purposes in confronting Rochester before leaving Thornfield are multiple, even contradictory, as I have suggested. First, she protects her identity as beloved woman, a tricky project as it is largely in Rochester's hands. Second, she wrestles with passion, her own and Rochester's: Is passion the threat to true love that she suspects? Third, she must re-examine the nature of her love for Rochester; if his Byronic adventurism is the key to his sexiness, will her moralizing kill it cold – or, worse yet, will his tale of virile conquests (not fit for an innocent's ears) enchant and enchain her conscience? Fourth, she's back on the marriage market, with more experience under her belt and a number of enticing, if unrespectable, offers from Rochester that put up for discussion all the terms of male–female moral relations. Last, is her feminist insistence on her own moral terms for her life, and the question of whether they can survive present circumstances. She is back in her most familiar dilemma, first encountered at Gateshead: '*Speak* I must: I had been trodden on severely, and *must* turn: but how?' (*38*).

Rochester's motives, on the other hand, remain quite Byronically simple: to keep Jane, to win her over into his loving, but still rakish, keeping, to make her a kept woman, sold to that happiness.

Rochester's first move, as we have seen, was to ask for forgiveness, his second to reassure Jane that he'll love her if mad, because she's different from Bertha. His third is to offer Jane the title of Mrs Rochester and a villa in the south of France, 'a secure sanctuary from hateful reminiscences, from unwelcome intrusion – even from falsehood and slander' (*304*). Bertha will be locked up even more securely, Adèle sent to school, both charges apparently dispensible: 'What do I want with a child for a companion? and not my own child, – a French dancer's bastard' (*304*). Rochester renounces his sinful past by buying it off, yet the future he offers Jane is unreconstructed, aristocratic double-dealing, also bought. Jane is not fooled. 'If I lived with you as you desire, I should then be your mistress: to say otherwise is sophistical – is false' (*306*).

Rochester's response to Jane's calm moralizing is virile violence, which brings out the angel in Jane:

'Jane! will you hear reason?' (he stopped and approached his lips to my ear) 'because, if you won't, I'll try violence.' His voice was hoarse; his look that of a man who is just about to burst an insufferable bond and plunge headlong into wild licence. I saw that in another moment, and with one impetus of frenzy more, I should be able to do nothing with him. The present – the passing second of time – was all I had in which to control and restrain him: a movement of repulsion, flight, fear, would have sealed my doom, – and his. But I was not afraid: not in the least.

I felt an inward power; a sense of influence, which supported me. The crisis was perilous; but not without its charm. . . .I took hold of his clenched hand; loosened the contorted fingers; and said to him, soothingly . . . (*304–5*)

And later:

'Jane, I am not a gentle-tempered man – you forget that: I am not long-enduring; I am not cool and dispassionate. Out of pity to me and yourself, put your finger on my pulse, feel how it throbs, and – beware!

He bared his wrist, and offered it to me: the blood was forsaking his cheek and lips, they were growing livid; I was distressed on all hands. To agitate him thus deeply by a resistance he so abhorred, was cruel: to yield was out of the question. I did what human beings do instinctively when they are driven to utter extremity – looked for aid to one higher than man: the words 'God help me' burst involuntarily from my lips. (*306*)

The morality play here highlights 'feminine reason and gentleness over masculine intolerance and violence'. As we shall see, her feminist subtext is that 'Free women would be the bearers of a new moral culture. Fettered women, on the other hand, were mental and moral cripples who contaminated all those around them.' Jane's feminism follows the ideas put forth by socialist feminists in the 1830s and 1840s, described by Barbara Taylor in her study, *Eve and the New Jerusalem*. 'The dilemma could only be resolved, as some Owenites realized, by postulating the simultaneous transformation of *both* sexes – the critique of a socially-defined femininity must become a critique of masculinity as well' (Taylor, 1983a: 31). And it does, in Jane's capable hands.

Jane's 'rational' insistence to the 'emotional' Rochester that (*1*) she does love him but (*2*) she is leaving him, clearly announces her own motives in the affair, which she sticks to while Rochester presents his last, best case: Jane has redeemed him from his fallen state; his lost and sinning ways were all for lack of an angel in his life.

The original sin was his father's, Rochester begins. As an

'avaricious, grasping man... it was his resolution to keep the property together' (*307*) for his older son Rowland, while finding a wealthy marriage for his younger son. The two morally bankrupt aristocrats arrange a cynically exploitative marriage for the innocent Rochester, who was 'dazzled, stimulated' by the beautiful time-bomb Bertha and the steamy tropical nights of Spanish Town, Jamaica, where colonialist fantasies of playing civilized/uncivilized with the natives apparently come true. 'My senses were excited; and being ignorant, raw, and inexperienced, I thought I loved her' (*307*). All the elements of aristocratic decay conspire in Rochester's ruin: greedy English patriarch sells his younger son for a £30,000 dowry into bondage with a colonial planter's daughter (already a step down) who is a half Creole, through her mother, not to mention more than half-mad: poorly bred, in other words. His senses tricked by her dark beauty, Rochester falls the 'romantic fall': the adventurer's lust betrays him to the empire's exotic Other, who by definition has no place in rational, civilized society where rules 'the law given by God; sanctioned by man' (*319*). Once married, Rochester wakes from his 'prurience,... rashness, the blindness of youth' (faults, really, not sins: a boy learning how to be a boy). What was once (in eighteenth-century romance) a free ride for wild rich youth is now (in nineteenth-century realism) a costly error that throws Rochester's 'spent fortune' into his governess's practical and morally impeccable bourgeois hands.

What Rochester wakes to see in the woman lying beside him is her total lack of civilised qualities: she simply isn't English, or middle-class. Need we list her faults of unwifeliness, unfitness as Rochester's equal? Rochester does, to show that he deserves better – Jane herself – that quintessential model of English bourgeois virtue – the governess.

'Bertha Mason, – the true daughter of an infamous mother,... a wife at once intemperate and unchaste' (*308–9*). 'I found her nature wholly alien to mine; her tastes obnoxious to me; her cast of mind common, low, narrow, and singularly incapable of being led to anything higher, expanded to anything larger', her conversation 'at once coarse and trite, perverse and imbecile ... I perceived that I should never have a quiet or settled household, because no servant would bear the continued outbreaks of her violent and unreasonable temper, or the vexations of her absurd, contradictory, exacting orders' (*308*). Aristocratic vices of drinking and adultery and abuse of servants are unchecked by any of the virtues learned through a sound (middle-class female's) education. The woman is a virtual weed, a home-grown, tropical passion-weed: 'Her character ripened and developed with frightful rapidity; her vices sprang up fast and rank' (*308*). Vices arise from character, character from nature, and Bertha's was 'a nature the most gross, impure, depraved I ever saw' (*309*). Rotten at the very core, this woman. Should any further proof of Bertha's overpowering, gigantic unsuitability (and Rochester's helplessness in the face of it) be required, it is supplied in Rochester's climactic clincher. Although Rochester inherits his father's and brother's estates when they die, he remains 'poor' because permanently unfulfilled, childless, and sapped by that black hole Bertha.

> 'And I could not rid myself of it by any legal proceedings: for the doctors now discovered that *my wife* was mad – her excesses had prematurely developed the germs of insanity: – Jane, you don't like my narrative; you look almost sick – shall I defer the rest to another day?'
> 'No sir, finish it now: I pity you – I do earnestly pity you'. (*309*)

Rochester stops at his familiar punch line to mark his story's effect, and this time elicits a sign of its success: female pities helpless male. Hardly headline news, unfortunately, but a key to where Jane now stands in relation to Rochester's nearly worn-out story: *with* him.

Earlier in the course of their romance, when Rochester had entertained, in a manner seduced Jane with his half-told tales of exotic sinning in foreign capitals, he had characterized his 'wrong tack at the age of one and twenty' (*138*) as the result of 'an error' – 'Mind, I don't say a crime' (*220*) – made 'when fate wronged me' (*139*). Then, as now, he had hedged his own responsiblity in the matter. He had asked Jane, a bit salaciously, to imagine herself in his circumstances: 'a wild boy indulged from childhood upwards; imagine yourself in a remote foreign land; conceive that you there commit a capital error ... not speaking of shedding of blood or any other guilty act ...' (*220*). He half jokes about his half-serious moral responsibility in the matter: 'I started, or rather (for, like other defaulters, I like to lay half the blame on ill fortune and adverse circumstances) was thrust on to a wrong tack at the age of one and twenty, and have never recovered the right course since' (*138*). 'When fate wronged me, I had not the wisdom to remain cool: I turned desperate; then I degenerated' (*139*).

Under discussion, obviously, is the problem of Rochester's past, inconveniently embodied in the unbudgable bodies of Bertha and Adèle. 'What exactly is his responsibility to these women?' Jane might well ask. These two beauties were reaped in foreign capitals from Rochester's sowing of wild oats. One caught in a Caribbean fever, the other conceived when Rochester was blinded by the footlights of a Parisian stage. But wait! Just as his father and brother had wronged him, and then his wife had turned inside out on him, so, too, his mistress, Adèle's mother, betrayed him. Not only did she have another lover, to whom Rochester heard her confess she didn't love Rochester – and he paying the bills! – but she lied about his paternity. All are veritable venereal diseases of a prostitute corrupting Rochester's pitiful, illicit love. The cure in the cases of both Bertha and Adèle is England, and Jane. 'Jane, from being a governess to a child becomes governess to a man and governess to the nation,' as Jina Politi brilliantly explains in her essay '*Jane Eyre* Class-ified' (Politi, 1982:65).

The cure for the 'fiery West Indian night' of the soul that suffocates Rochester in 'air ... like sulphur-steams' is 'a wind fresh from Europe ... the storm broke ... and the air grew pure. ... "Go," said Hope, "and live again in Europe,"' free from Bertha's blight on your reputation and night's sleep. '"See that she is cared for as her condition demands, and you have done all that God and Humanity require of you"' (*311*).

The cure for his subsequent European sins, Rochester says, is

Adèle's English upbringing, which he initiated when:

> the mother ... abandoned her child and ran away to Italy with a
> musician or singer. I acknowledged no natural claim on Adèle's
> part to be supported by me; nor do I now acknowledge any, for I
> am not her father; but hearing that she was quite destitute, I e'en
> took the poor thing out of the slime and mud of Paris, and
> transplanted it here, to grow up clean in the wholesome soil of
> an English country garden. Mrs Fairfax found you to train it. ...
> (*147-8*)

Inasmuch as Rochester was 'foolish' enough to waste his
legacy amongst undeservingly materialistic foreigners, he is to
blame; his *error* – mind, I don't say *crime* – is 'virility rampant'.
Inasmuch as he acknowledges that the cure lies at home in the
hands of God and Jane Eyre, he's almost home free. That is,
Rochester's and Jane's common moral ground is this sense of
nationalist and racial superiority, with its domestic counter-
parts, 'fallen', European-style, aristocrat male, and 'risen',
English, educated, middle-class female. Race, class, and gender
are all implicated in Jane Eyre's feminist–triumph–in-the-
making. Rochester's past, in the process, is transformed from
inert burden to the very 'matter' of his spiritual transformation,
the material he will re-view according to the new God-fearing
moral perspective Jane is about to teach him. His version and
Jane's already agree on the race and class dynamic of spiritual
virtuosity; he seems to agree on the gender dynamic, that Jane is
his pure girl saviour, he 'not a villain', just 'trite common-place
Sinner, hackneyed in all the poor petty dissipations with which
the rich and worthless try to put on life' (*138*). Now he will be
'healed and cleansed, with a very angel as my comforter' (*262*).
'All the ground I have wandered over shall be re-trodden by
you: wherever I stamped my hoof, your sylph's foot shall step
also' (*262*). This last bit is his delusion, that he gets to be the
satyr and Jane has to be the (bodiless) fairy sprite; that Jane can
redeem his past. Tempting, and empowering for Jane to believe
so, and in accord with the conventional cementwork of male-
need–female–service that is still the bedrock of gender relations.
    But. Jane's 'but' is the most powerful word in her growing

vocabulary, creating the most powerful moment in her life story. Her very voice – ability to speak – and act – leaving Rochester – hang on one 'but'. What is that 'but' that prohibits her from staying with the love of her life? Few readers of the novel would stand there with Jane, make that choice against love.

Jane's point is that Rochester must redeem his own past, she cannot be used to wipe out his sins with her purity, like some sort of eraser. His arrogance hopes that he and she can manipulate the terms of his spiritual penitence. Her fantasy, which she suppresses, is that her ambitious claim of moral superiority can rewrite 'the law given by God; sanctioned by man', the (holiest of holy, apparently) law of holy matrimony.

Rochester tempts Jane with all the temptations that romance holds for women: to fulfil all the needs unfulfilled in real life, where femininity demands self-denial and subordination. Rochester's retelling of his life story becomes a classic romance, Rochester the lost and hopeless hero, Jane the patient and charmingly innocent heroine waiting at the end of his unfulfilling travels for him to recognize her as home. Rochester reruns the plot of Jane's Thornfield chapters – but from *his* point of view – and instead of the doubts plaguing Jane about Rochester's motives and her own temptations to 'fall' into love, instead of Jane's unconscious struggles over passion and purity intricately shadow-danced with Bertha, instead of the troublesome female version of romance, where sexuality and subordination are problems forever to be grappled with, we are given the unproblemmatical male version of romance, a smooth-running and unambiguous plot of attraction, evaluation, seduction, and salvation. 'I came, I saw, I conquered', as Rochester seems to see it; and finally 'I was conquered'. That is Rochester's munificent concession to Jane's feminism, which, not incidentally, serves his every self-interest in claiming Jane as his saviour.

His version of the romance has its attractions for Jane, by simultaneously providing vicarious and self-righteous thrills of conquest. Here he had tried tropical passion, he had tried European courtesans, all to no avail.

My fixed desire was to seek and find a good and intelligent woman, whom I could love.... For ten long years I roved about, living first in one capital, then another.... Provided with plenty of money, and the passport of an old name, I could choose my own society: no circles were closed to me. I sought my ideal woman amongst English ladies, French countesses, Italian signoras, and German Gräfinnen. I could not find her.... Yet I could not live alone; so I tried the companionship of mistresses. The first I chose was Céline Varens.... She had two successors: an Italian, Giacinta, and a German, Clara; both considered singularly handsome. *(312–14)*

We know what's coming, don't we, girls? 'And then I found *you*.' But play it again, Sam, stretch it out about your 'harsh, bitter frame of mind, the result of a useless, roving, lonely life' *(314)*. Describe your despair: 'for I began to regard the notion of an intellectual, faithful, loving woman as a mere dream' *(314)*. And renounce your past as a mistake you'll never repeat again:

It was a grovelling fashion of existence: I should never like to return to it. Hiring a mistress is the next worse thing to buying a slave: both are often by nature, and always by position, inferior: and to live familiarly with inferiors is degrading. I now hate the recollection of the time I passed with Céline, Giacinta, and Clara. *(314)*

In playing this particular card of the game of romance, necessary to prove that Jane taught him 'true love' and he now sees the degradation of illicit love, Rochester concedes perhaps more than he knows at this moment. He seems to think that 'rake's reform' is merely a matter of a sincere telling of the old tale to a captive audience, with all the juicy bits piously re-captioned. He is still the silver-tongued devil, but about to be hoisted on his own petard, because Jane has a feminist flash about Rochester's opinion of his mistresses. What woman hasn't felt that subversive twinge when some poor girls are desecrated at the expense of some rake's 'reform'?

Jane realizes the necessity of her own self-protection from such slavery to love, really a fate of prostitution for women outside marriage. 'If I were so far to forget myself ... to become the successor to these poor girls, he would one day regard me with the same feeling which now in his mind desecrates their memory' *(314)*. She's femininely protecting her identity as beloved woman, but she's not collaborating in his judgment against the women as bad, necessarily. It's *his* feeling that desecrates their memory. Rather, she sees with feminist clarity how the double standard victimizes women. Mistresses have no power, and *she'd lose all her power with her purity*, and with that, all Rochester's love. These are radical connections Jane makes, between male control of the terms of love and male control of the terms of female sexuality. It's a neonatal critique of the double standard as part of the bulwark of patriarchy. Significantly, Jane 'did not give utterance to this conviction: it was enough to feel it. I impressed it on my heart, that it might remain there to serve me as aid in the time of trial' *(314)*. An ace-in-the-hole, this realization of Jane's that Rochester's terms for her, whether as angel or as 'superior' mistress, or pretend wife, are really the same as his terms for the other women in his life; she *doesn't* get a better deal than the double standard, no matter how cleverly he insists otherwise. The rake's reform goes no deeper than renouncing the bad for the good woman. The double standard for male conduct and female conduct remains, as does the good/bad woman dichotomy. Jane's feminism questions Rochester's power to label and buy bad women through prostitution and a good woman through marriage, while assuming his own right to both sexual experience and the 'pure' status of marriage.

At this moment in his story where he renounces hiring mistresses, Rochester suspects he has not secured Jane's belief in the rake's reform: 'You disapprove of me still, I see. But let me come to the point' *(314)* – the point being Jane, playing his good angel. What Rochester has quietly conceded here, however, is half Jane's battle. Change the stress of his confession slightly, and see what he has acknowledged: he was degraded by his master/slave lovenests. *He*? Mr Lonelyhearts, Mr Love-the-one-you're-with? He was degraded by illicit and materialistic love? His idea of degradation – 'to live familiarly with inferiors is degrading' – sounds more like an aristocratic distaste for intimacy with the lower orders, than an acknowledgment that his exploitation of women makes him a real heel. But it's a start. It's another ace-in-the-hole for Jane, because it shows that male power does not control all the terms of moral censure. Sexual degradation is a two-edged sword, properly handled. Men, too, can be degraded by their sexual conduct; men, too, can be held accountable for it; men can pay their own way into moral responsibility. No more free rides on women's backs! No more blaming Bertha for your tropical heat, or Adèle and Céline for your slumming with showgirls. No more using Jane's goodness to justify your attempt at bigamy, or your own despair to blackmail Jane into saving your ass. Free all prisoners of sex! Catch the real criminals and prosecute them to the fullest extent of the law. Not the double-standard law, but the single standard of marital co-responsibility. Let him rattle on, then spring the trap and hold Mr Sex Life hostage to his own tale!

Rochester makes his final offer, and it's hung on a powerfully flattering portrait of Jane. He really knows how to work the pivotal point of romance: the surly fallen male uplifted on the wings of an angel. When he first saw Jane, when she first 'looked and spoke with a sort of authority' and offered him her hand (he's fallen off his horse, remember), 'When once I had pressed the frail shoulder, something new – a fresh sap and sense – stole into my frame' (*315*). This is the workings of 'true love', promising a miraculous healing power over the fallen male, which culminates in 'perfect union':

> After a youth and manhood passed half in unutterable misery and half in dreary solitude, I have for the first time found what I can truly love – I have found *you*. You are my sympathy – my better self – my good angel – I am bound to you with a strong attachment. I think you good, gifted, lovely: a fervent, a solemn passion is conceived in my heart; it leans to you, draws you to my centre and spring of life, wraps my existence about you – and, kindling in pure, powerful flame, fuses you and me in one. (*317*)

This is some marriage proposal – good enough for most girls, better than any real confession I've ever heard of male need for female moral service.

How tempted is Jane?

> I was experiencing an ordeal: a hand of fiery iron grasped my vitals. Terrible moment: full of struggle, blackness, burning! Not a human being that ever lived could wish to be loved better than I was loved; and him who thus loved me I absolutely worshipped: and I must renounce love and idol. *(318)*

Here is Jane's answer to all who think that she's a fool for love, because women will do anything for love, women believe love can solve everything.

In her final speech, Jane makes her definitive declaration of independence from love and Rochester and romance, from 'the silken fetters of desire' that imprison women in emotional dependency, from all the subordination and self-denial demanded by conventional femininity, and from her role in the rake's-reform hypocrisy of sexual double-dealing. Rochester asks her:

> 'Is it better to drive a fellow-creature to despair than to transgress a mere human law – no man being injured by the breach? for you have neither relatives nor acquaintances whom you need fear to offend by living with me.'
>
> This was true: and while he spoke my very conscience and reason turned traitors against me, and charged me with crime in resisting him. They spoke almost as loud as Feeling: and that clamoured wildly. 'Oh comply!' it said. 'Think of his misery; think of his danger – look at his state when left alone; remember his headlong nature; consider the recklessness following on despair – soothe him; save him; love him; tell him you love him and will be his. Who in the world cares for *you*? or who will be injured by what you do?'
>
> Still indomitable was the reply – '*I* care for myself. The more solitary, the more friendless, the more unsustained I am, the more I will respect myself. I will keep the law given by God; sanctioned by man. I will hold to the principles received by me when I was sane, and not mad – as I am now. Laws and principles are not for the times when there is no temptation: they are for such moments as this, when body and soul rise in mutiny against their rigour; stringent are they; inviolate they shall be. If

at my individual convenience I might break them, what would be their worth? They have a worth – so I have always believed; and if I cannot believe it now, it is because I am insane – quite insane: with my veins running fire, and my heart beating faster than I can count its throbs. Preconceived opinions, foregone determinations, are all I have at this hour to stand by; there I plant my foot.' *(319)*

Individual conscience is Jane's final arbiter in the matter, and it rules that matrimony is not a transgressable social boundary, and principles are a woman's real source of self-respect and her sole friends in her hour of greatest vulnerability.

Jane's 'governessness' here comes to her aid. She can figure and draw the moral from the lesson, using a heroic amount of patience and self-control in the face of unruliness threatening a violent usurpation. Her single-womanhood and protestant individualism define her conscience. If she had pinned her all on romance, she could die now of despair, or follow Rochester into the 'miry wilds whence there is no extrication' *(163)*, or just hang around as she has been, the prim governess watching the upper class destroy itself in extramarital excesses of dissipation and debauchery. But Jane refuses these plots of romance.

Instead, she 'plants her foot' on the firm ground of domestic feminism, where passion is subdued by the spirit, in man as well as woman. No double standard in Jane Eyre's household. And if Jane's going to give up *her* romantic fantasy of passion-meeting-passion in ecstatic oblivion, well Rochester is, too, going to have to give up *his* romantic fantasy of fallen male free-loading off female purity. He's going to have to go through the same struggle Jane did over passion and purity, wrestle with his own Bertha-figure, and subdue all the desires that *have no place* in marriage.

The most radical renovation of Jane's feminist triumph is Rochester's coming round at last to Jane's sense of morality as an inviolable integrity of spirit that cannot be seduced by love or lust, or need or violence, or trickery or intimidation. He admits she's won. Her power withstands his attempts at mastery. 'He seemed to devour me with his flaming glance: physically, I felt, at the moment, powerless as stubble exposed to the draught and glow of a furnace – mentally, I still possessed my soul, and with it the certainty of ultimate safety' (*320*). Jane stares him down.

> 'Never', said he, as he ground his teeth, 'never was anything at once so frail and so indomitable.... Consider that eye; consider the resolute, wild, free thing looking out of it, defying me, with more than courage – with a stern triumph. Whatever I do with its cage, I cannot get at it – the savage, beautiful creature! If I tear, if I rend the slight prison, my outrage will only let the captive loose. Conqueror I might be of the house; but the inmate would escape to heaven before I could call myself possessor of its clay dwelling-place. And it is you, spirit – with will and energy, and virtue and purity – that I want: not alone your brittle frame. Of yourself, you could come with soft flight and nestle against my heart, if you would: seized against your will you will elude the grasp like an essence – you will vanish ere I inhale your fragrance. Oh! come, Jane, come!' (*320*)

Jane's spirit still looks like a bird in Rochester's eyes, but not the singing little linnet that first 'hopped to my foot and proposed to bear me on its tiny wing' (*315*) all tweety tweet and gravely sweet. This bird is savage, beautiful, resolute, wild, and free, at once frail and indomitable. This bird has a will of its own that can elude the grasp of Rochester; it will not come when he calls. This bird, lacking all feminine grace, refuses to soothe or save him.

More, this 'thing' has defied Rochester, with more than courage, more than effort; it has sternly triumphed over him and his outrage, his attempts to get at it, to conquer and possess it. His manly efforts have not worked, and why not? What is *this* woman's essence that eludes his sure grasp?

Finally and clearly he sees the thing 'it'self in Jane, that is her essence and the source of his love for her: 'And it is you, spirit – with will and energy, and virtue and purity – that I want: not alone your brittle frame' (*320*). Possession of this woman's body slides away to secondary interest, and with it all Rochester's power and presumption as a rake. His old vision, belief, strength, and power all seep away and fade as if illusions, or lusty dreams that evaporate and leave his hands agonizingly empty and grasping at what once fed. Now *he* is cast on the cold hillside, alone and palely loitering.

Rochester now sees that this woman's spirit is a mightier prize than her body – so mighty as to be priceless, unpossessable. The female body that once defined the terms of Rochester's mastery – the coin of his realm – becomes mere clay in his hands, brittle to his touch, inert, lifeless, inanimate. Rochester's belief in his own savage power over quiveringly malleable female flesh is nightmarishly inverted in his dawning vision of this 'new woman'. He sees in her an *active* (masculine) will and energy, electrifying what he had believed to be a passive (feminine) virtue and purity. She has all the power forged from passion and purity, strength and tenderness, wildness and resolution. She does not lack whatever most women seem to lack and seek in men. His command, his virility, his masterful stare and presumptive authority and forceful body, all his masculine power is cancelled by this indomitable spirit that, he sees, has integrated the complementary virtues of male and female.

And, best news last, when Rochester says, 'And it is you, spirit, that I want', he shows the glimmerings of a new desire, a new appreciation of value, and a beginning of understanding of the workings of the spirit. Jane has really taught him a lot. 'Wanting you' is the most common coin of the realm in romance, and superficially it is the desire that seeks 'possession' of the other, howsoever that is understood, or, perhaps more frequently misunderstood between the sexes. In Rochester's old terms, 'wanting you' has the gentlemanly meaning of marriage, but this being now impossible, it has the slightly less gallant meaning of 'all-but-married', pseudo-marital relations, whose social meaning Jane has already figured out.

But 'it is you, spirit, that I want' suggests as well a whole other – a *spiritual* realm of desire, where possession, if possible at all, is not possible physically or legally or socially, but must be, somehow, spiritual, and where the 'wanting' can be for intimacy, communion, understanding, the rare moment when 'It is my spirit that addresses your spirit.' We are back to Jane's 'marriage proposal' in the garden that midsummer's eve, when

Jane discounts her social and physical identity, 'poor, obscure, plain and little', in favour of her spiritual and emotional equality to Rochester:

> I have full as much soul as you, – and full as much heart! ... I am not talking to you now through the medium of custom, conventionalities, or even of mortal flesh: – it is my spirit that addresses your spirit; just as if both had passed through the grave, and we stood at God's feet, equal, – as we are! (255)

Possession, Jane knows as a teacher, is less a matter of transferring ownership as it is a matter of engendering ability, the power to be and do for oneself instead of seeking the other for that power. Rochester's vision of Jane's integrity of spirit sets in motion his own salvation, his sole responsibility for his own spirit: a strict accountancy with God, rather than a seduction-transaction with a saving angel.

Jane's transformation of desire, from fleshly and materialistic appetite, to spiritual communion and accountability, transforms by magic the inequalities of class and gender between Jane and Rochester. Qualities of mind and soul – the powers of an educated woman – prove more than equal to the shallow show of social snobbery and the self-devouring demands of unchecked aristocratic appetite. Leaving Thornfield, Jane has triumphed over Blanche and Bertha, Rochester's rakehood and his cheap version of reformed rakehood, and over her own passions and archaic romance fantasies of love-conquers-all and angel-saves-sinner. *As governess*, cultivated mind over un-schooled feelings, Jane secures the victory of middle-class woman's moral superiority over the fallen worldly male.

Charlotte Brontë reveals her ambition for all women to achieve such a victory as Jane Eyre's, in a letter she wrote in the same period in which she was writing the novel. In response to Ellen Nussey's tale of Joe Taylor's multiple flirtations in the neighbourhood, she replied:

> This is an unfair state of things; the match is not equal. I only wish I had the power to infuse into the soul of the persecuted a little of the quiet strength of pride – of the supporting conscious-

ness of superiority (for they are superior to him because purer) –
of the fortifying resolve of firmness to bear the present and wait.
Could all the virgin population of Birstall and Gomersall
receive and retain these sentiments, Joe Taylor would eventually
have to vail his crest before them.

(Peters, 1986: 192)

Pride in such womanly purity did not exactly come naturally to
Jane Eyre, or without cost. Bertha teaches Jane the feminist
lesson of romance: only female purity can tame male demand,
and only at the cost of female desire. When Bertha comes out of
the gothic closet where female fiction and desire have free play,
into the glare of the real world's prohibitive social meanings for
female appetite, all Bertha's power as unknown Other is spent –
but spent well: her legacy to Jane is secure. She has given Jane
the critical difference in view from outside romance, the
motherly spirit that asks the tough questions about the power
relations governing romantic male protectorship of female
innocence. By incorporating Bertha's revisionary perspective,
Jane has found a way to make purity the impassioned moral
agency that is a woman's power in the household.

Chapter Three

HEAVENLY FATHER

T HE man of feeling, straight out of the pages of romantic fiction, having failed her, perhaps the man of reason, straight out of the Church of England (not to mention Haworth Parsonage), might be made to do. St John Rivers, as every reader of the novel experiences, is saintly to a fault, to such a moralizing and self-righteous degree that reading about his conflict and courtship with Jane is as tedious an exercise in self-punishment for the reader, as the Thornfield chapters were heart-throbbingly self-indulgent. Much of the vitality goes out of the novel when Jane leaves behind the man and wife who did so much to enchant and educate her senses and her under- standing about love and sex. Everything she is to learn about men and marriage from St John Rivers is drab and dutiful, exacting and self-denying, claustrophobic and constricting. Moor House is the story of a daughter's subordination to a patriarch of a father with a religious whip in his hands, God Himself as his witness, and a stone for a heart when it comes to Jane Eyre as a woman. He tries to teach her her place as a dutiful daughter: to minister to the father's needs and obey His commands without question or complaint, but also without witholding or losing any of the intellectual and spiritual power that makes her so worthy to serve Him. His challenge is to bend her to His will without breaking her spirit: a parent's and a teacher's trickiest tightrope between love and self-love.

Ever a caviller and a questioner, Jane can be counted on to uncover the hypocrisy and corruptions of power at the heart of religious and family duty as expertly as she did the stubborn double standard at the heart of romance and rake's reform. The differences will be seen to be as crucial as the similarities between these female fates of enthralment. One is to the rakish hero, the man of romantically inspired feeling, a hero fed by fiction and imagination. The other is to the father, the man of institutionally backed reason, a master fed by fact and real life. One proves educable and offers a future of domestic equality for Jane, the other definitively blocks the door to her future, demanding her subordination and pointing to the social world that reinforces his control of her destiny. Is it any wonder that Jane hears Rochester's woeful cry to her just as St John ejaculates, 'My prayers are heard!' and lays his hand more firmly on her head and surrounds her with his fatherly embrace? She chooses love over duty, not so much as a girl chooses reading romance novels over the washing of her father's socks, but as a woman chooses the space where female power, choice, and authority have effect, over the space where the patriarch lays down the law for every move and thought, and every contradictory desire hides quivering or dies shivering of the cold. St John's power over Jane is finally limited by his limited capacity for love, for feeling, and thus for moral growth, and Jane's power is finally 'in play and in force', as she puts its, because of her capacity to feel and recognize love when it inspires moral authority and when it does not. 'I knew the difference,' she says, and breaks the spell of duty cast over the daughter like an iron shroud.

Having sighted the light at the end of Jane's Moor House tunnel – the beacon in her dark wilderness of self-denial – we can pause to ask more particularly what draws Jane into the psychosocial economy of the Rivers family, and how it works, without the reader's acute anxiety that she will get stuck in Marsh End, 'Moor-Housed' to death. Our boredom with and chafing against the last third of the novel may well be caused in large part by our own anxieties about (a mother's) 'slow-death-by-domestic-sphere', (a wife's) self-suffocation by loveless duty, and (a daughter's) starvation from stingy fatherliness (too little love and approval to live on). Charlotte Brontë's conjuring of the tormented self-divisions of romance within Jane at Thornfield read like an expansive gothicized adventure tale. The excruciating self-division of a family romance from the pubescent female's point of view reads more like a tract, that stealthily contracts the horizon and that uplifts in a spirit that is actually down-dragging all the way. Unlike marriage, family is neither chosen nor negotiable, and proves a dead-end for Jane's feminist ambitions and desires.

Leaving Gateshead via the red room, leaving Lowood via the advice of 'a kind fairy', leaving Thornfield via the moon-mother, Jane's exits are supernaturally instigated and blessed by some kind of benevolent mother figure who supports Jane's best and boldest impulses when she is most isolated, when her judgment is most in danger of being repudiated by propriety. Adrienne Rich (1979) traces this feminist support system in her 'early' essay on *Jane Eyre*, 'The temptations of a motherless woman', first published in *Ms.* magazine in 1973. Rather than stress the mystical as motive, however, I would point out how *social* are the problems that propel Jane from place to place.

Beginning again in each new situation, Jane's isolation is emphasized – as caused by her nature and situation as an orphan, unmarried, educated woman. The 'Portrait of a Governess, disconnected, poor, and plain' is redrawn on blank paper each time she embarks anew, showing how she must prove her very self to others to win her right to exist as the dependant she has no choice but to be: to be fed and clothed by them in return for her work as student, later teacher. In night-marish repetition, John Reed's patriarchal prophesy of dispos-session comes true:

> You have no business to take our books; you are a dependant . . .;
> you have no money; your father left you none; you ought to beg,
> and not to live here with gentlemen's children like us, and eat
> the same meals we do, and wear clothes at our mama's expense.
> *(12–13)*

In fairy-talelike repetition Jane will magically transform dis-inheritance into inheritance, and like a Fury disguised as fairy godmother, avenge the unavenged injustices against her as dispossessed woman.

When she leaves Thornfield Jane has less than ever before, including uncharacteristically weak knees and a short attention span. She falls, she crawls on her hands and knees, she leaves her tiny purse behind in the coach. She has no references, connections, or prospects. 'And now,' she proclaims like Bunyan's pilgrim entering the wilderness, 'I am absolutely destitute' (*325*). Spiritually, of course, this is an asset and not a liability.

Psychically, Jane always has some fuel left in her tank, but materially and therefore socially she has, as John Reed so bluntly put it, nothing. 'I was brought face to face with Necessity. I stood in the position of one without a resource: without a friend; without a coin' (*328*). Necessity is played by a series of 'mild-looking, cleanly-attired' working-class house-wives, and servants, and shopclerks, from whom Jane seeks work. 'Who employs women?' she asks. 'Are there any jobs as servant or needlewoman?' No. And the farms and factory employ only men. 'And what do the women do?' 'I knawn't,' was the answer. 'Some does one thing, and some another. Poor folk mun get on as they can' (*329*). Jane sees suspicion in each working woman's face: 'in her eyes, how doubtful must have appeared my character, position, tale' (*329*). Politely unspoken, the assumption is that a lady fallen to begging must have been cast out, deservedly outcast. 'And the white door closed, quite gently and civilly: but it shut me out' (*329*). Ladyhood is supported by propriety, Jane sees, and without it – without anyone to recognize it in her – she's as lost as 'a lost and starving dog' (*330*). Dependants look comfortable enough when attached to the skirts of family life, but cut loose they are mortally helpless to help – to 'keep' – themselves. When the net of gentility is rent, the fall to destitution and death could be as quick as three days, in Jane's case.

Luckily, St John hears her prayers, picks her up off her knees, and wrests her grovelling gratitude for her survival from God's hands to his own. Jane's male-rescue fantasy begins again (sigh), but as before, it is a pragmatic and not an escapist solution to her real situation as a single woman in need of a way to earn her living. The men she 'conjures up' in such moments actually do provide her with the opportunities she needs for her future self-sufficiency (as hemmed in and dependent as it is for her as governess and teacher). Mr Reed, the apothecary, even Brocklehurst must 'approve' Jane's progress before promoting it; she cannot graduate from Gateshead nor enroll at Lowood without their recommendation. Men guard the door to women's education and work. What they are looking for in the woman they promote is called 'tractability' by St John, 'humility' by Brocklehurst, and 'discretion' by Rochester, a term of praise: 'that discretion I respect in you – with that foresight, prudence and humility which befit your responsible and dependent position' (252).

When such moralizing terms are actually articulated as the job qualifications that they are, we can see how 'narrow, and narrowing' (356) are the doors through which 'Plain Jane' progresses. There's not much that's 'free, blank, "pre-social"' (Eagleton, 1975: 26) about Jane Eyre and her progress, contrary to so much critical opinion. As an orphan and single woman, untied to family, she may be even more caught in social propriety without a home of her own, since the men in her life determine which character traits, which behaviour, which goals, and which attitudes are supportable in Jane, and which are insupportable. And not just her progress, Jane learns when she quits without a reference as a governess: her very survival rests on St John's decision that she 'fits' his purposes. To experience such dependency on male authority, where even one's most intimate feelings about, say, Good, self-purity, ambition, are scrutinized and evaluated in narrowly righteous and patriarchal terms, is to get to the very bottom of women's oppression. This is Charlotte Brontë's feminist achievement in *Jane Eyre*: analyzing and struggling to redefine from inside the terms of women's love, work, and ambition, in all their great social and psychic detail. So rather than beating Jane Eyre and Charlotte Brontë over the head with such clubs as 'sado-masochism', 'lovesick', and 'pathology' as the determinants of their suffering – hardly necessary if they do enjoy doing it to themselves, eh? – let us see whether the causes of Jane's broken heart might lie beyond some innate impulse to stick pins in her eyes.

Emotionally, Jane's resources are divided, her loyalty to self even at the base level of survival being chewed at by the weight of Rochester's authority for her. Self-doubt, with a killer instinct, threatens her very identity: 'What was I? In the midst of my pain of heart, and frantic effort of principle, I abhorred myself. I had no solace from self-approbation: none even from self-respect. I had injured – wounded – left my master' (*323*). In leaving her master Jane injures and wounds her*self*, her own heart 'plained of its gaping wounds, its inward bleeding, its riven chords' (*326*). Love, yes, but love, as we learned at Thornfield, is not unmixed with learning, power, morality. Jane, too polite to mention it even to herself, has challenged and overcome her master in the struggle over the moral terms of their relationship, and he conceded her power, crowned her with praise. Once more, her ambition has usurped her master's place in her heart's hierarchy, and as with John Reed, and in Frances Henri's poem in Charlotte Brontë's novel *The Professor*, the student's success brings an unbreachable ocean between them and breaks open a 'secret bleeding inward wound' in her heart where his protection and authority used to nestle (Peters, 1986:186).

Winning integrity at the cost of love is so radically unfeminine it stands on its head Sarah Lewis's *sine qua non* of *Woman's Mission* (1839): 'the one quality on which woman's value and influence depends is the renunciation of self' (Taylor, 1983a:124). Jane has successfully asserted self, articulated a morality challenging womanly self-denial at the service of male need. Jane's action, not Fate, and not Bertha, is 'the doom which had reft me from adhesion to my master' (*362*), leaving her alone with her conscience, lonely: 'I say *lonely*, for . . . visible to me, there was no building apparent save the church and the parsonage' (*362*). Her self-imposed exile at Moor House, recuperating from such self-indulgence with a stringent diet of self-denial, is her harsh means of testing the strength and validity of her alternative morality.

Her guilt at having 'wounded' Rochester and transgressed womanliness explains much of her subsequent indulgence in self-denial at the feet of another master. St John acts as a cold shower on romanticizing notions; he coldly commands where Rochester had desirously demanded, so he seems to be the objective authority that Jane needs after romance has proven an 'ignis fatuus' entrapping the susceptible. (Moor House, too, she first suspects is an ignis fatuus; and so it proves.)

Sexual guilt is no small part of Jane's transgression against the proprieties of courtship. Passion has been announced, indulged in, and integrated into her moral stand as a woman with 'full as much soul as you, ... and full as much heart!' Jane's nervy proposal to Rochester was provoked by passion, and it paid off handsomely. But after Bertha leapt out of the closet, such passion proved more dangerous than the naïve Jane might have hoped. She reads in Rochester's rakehood the degradations of illicit passion, and in Bertha the degradations of female sexuality itself. Seeing Bertha and Rochester wrestle on the floor of Thornfield's attic has overcast Jane's transcendent vision of marital passion with a very ugly literalness: Bertha on all fours and Rochester *hating her for it*. Rochester's past, Bertha's body, and Jane's imagination all need scrubbing down, and at Moor House, Jane goes to it with a vengeance.

> 'What aim, what purpose, what ambition in life do you have now?' [St John asks her].
> 'My first aim will be to *clean down* (do you comprehend the full force of the expression?) to *clean down* Moor House from chamber to cellar; my next to rub it up with beeswax, oil, and an indefinite number of cloths, till it glitters again; my third, to arrange every chair, table, bed, carpet, with mathematical precision.' (*392*)

With punishing blasts of breezy British common sense, self-reliance, and protestant self-denial, Jane will convince herself that Queen Victoria herself would approve her choice for God, country, and the self-supporting middle class:

> Whether it is better, I ask, to be a slave in a fool's paradise at

Marseilles – fevered with delusive bliss one hour – suffocating
with the bitterest tears of remorse and shame the next – or to be a
village-schoolmistress, free and honest, in a breezy mountain
nook in the healthy heart of England? (*362*)

Her material, social, and physical destitution turn out to be her
ticket into Moor House, signs of her spiritual readiness for a
complete overhaul. She scrubs herself clean when she arrives
after her dirtying ordeal: 'Purified and rendered presentable,'
she shows 'no speck of dirt, no trace of the disorder I so hated,
and which seemed so to degrade me, left' (*342*). This is adult
Victorian religious conscience of a kind that even Sarah Ellis
would approve: Cooks must wash hands before handling
family food, as the signs all say. Before joining those haloed
bluestocking sisters in their bookish parlour, such virgins of
sexual innocence after her dicey experiences, Jane must
straighten her collar and wipe the drool off her dress, so to
speak. Personal hygiene, as every American knows, is the only
remedy for sexual guilt! Jane is like an adolescent girl returning
home from a wild party, seeking bubble bath or even a cold
shower, 'good-girlishness' and Daddy's trust and protection,
'the fragrance of new bread, and the warmth of a generous fire'
(*342*). 'Home' may be – must be – the solution to the violence of
expectation and deceit and disillusionment fomenting between
the sexes in the world outside. If not 'fiancée', then 'daughter' is
the place safe from the transactions of the sexual marketplace.
The fantasy of fatherly rescue haunts Jane, for reasons she is to
explore and resolve before leaving the Rivers family.

'Going home' is not choice but necessity when a woman has
no work; it offers a spiritual solution to the problem of 'the
silken snare' of passion (*361*), and it provides an approved social
place and role as dutiful daughter, first, and second, as teacher.
And, most poignantly, home is where the heart is, the place
where Jane can be sure of recognition, approval, and love for
who she is, and not misunderstood, unseen, indifferently treated,
or subjected to the injustices meted out to women as women in
the world. ('This idea, consolatory in theory', like Jane's other
ideas about fulfilment, she learns after the fact is 'terrible if
realised' (*19*).

Heavenly Father

Indeed, *being recognized* is the key to Jane's and St John's growing intimacy and sense of common destiny. Over and over, each uncovers and addresses the other's secrets, vulnerabilities, and unrecognized needs, Jane whittling away at St John's resistance to passion (for Rosamund) and St John whittling away at Jane's resistance to duty. They have each other's number, because both are burning with ambition and thwarted passion, and determined to subdue both with as much cerebration as is required.

Jane recognizes St John's nature in herself, as a daughter might come to understand a father's legacy once she has been out in the world; then she comes to see the man's limitations, and finally how they limit her as long as she remains 'under the influence of the ever-watchful blue eye' (*399*).

First, Jane feels the gratitude of one who is recognized:

> Somehow, now that I had once crossed the threshold of this house, and once was brought face to face with its owners, I felt no longer outcast, vagrant, and disowned by the wide world. I dared to put off the mendicant – to resume my natural manner and character. I began once more to know myself. (*339*)

Family is the only place where Jane can put off the mendicant (the punishing role of single woman), ever an ill-fitting mask, and know herself through being known, that luxury of love.

The sisters recognize Jane through 'their spontaneous, genuine, genial compassion' (*350*), while St John's 'evangelical charity' (*350*) 'demanded an account' (*339*) before appropriating any funds. The generosity of women, flowing with feeling, under the stern and parsimonious supervision of 'a cold hard man', recalls Lowood's hierarchy, where school and church interlocked to ensure that education be chained to duty and lack of choice and horizon, not prized as ambition's ill-gotten gains.

Sustenance by the sisters' loving recognition of her is gratefully received and repaid by Jane, but all is stasis in the female sphere. Jane eats hearty – 'I devoured the books they lent me' (*352*) – then wants more, seeking recognition, approval, and opportunity for her ambition from the home's highest, not to mention only, authority. St John encourages her ambition:

'I hope you will begin to look beyond Moor House and Morton, and sisterly society, and the selfish calm and sensual comfort of civilised affluence. I hope your energies will then once more trouble you with their strength.'

... 'To what end?' [asks Jane]

'To the end of turning to profit the talents which God has commended to your keeping; and of which He will surely one day demand a strict account. Jane, I shall watch you closely ... I warn you of that.' *(393)*

Jane looks to St John as St John looked to his Father – but daughter and son do not receive quite the same legacy. The good daughter's legacy at Moor House is Eve's legacy in *Paradise Lost*: obedience to her lord and master Adam. Unlike Jane, Milton's Eve really knows her place:

My Author and Disposer, what thou bidd'st
Unargu'd I obey; so God ordains,
God is thy Law, thou mine: to know no more
Is woman's happiest knowledge and her praise.

(Gilbert and Gubar, 1979: 202)

St John's power – intellect, morality, confidence in his manifest destiny, and lust for power and renown – stems from welding his ambition to religion, and thus deriving his authority from the Father's as His Son. Familial, religious, and national paternalism speak as one in the parsonage. The Other in this discourse is by definition female, Roman Catholic, and Indian – or West Indian (Bertha) – or Greek, or Spaniard, as is explained by another Victorian ambitious for the Church of England, Charles Kingsley:

the highest idea of man is to know his Father, and to look his Father in the face, in full assurance of faith and love; and that out of that springs all manful energy, self-respect, all self-restraint, all that the true Englishman has, and the Greek and Spaniard have not ... if anyone wishes to benefit the poor whom God has committed to their charge, they must do anything and everything rather than go to Rome – to a creed ... [which] substitut[es] a Virgin Mary, who is to *nurse* them like infants, for a father in whom they are men and brothers.

(Harris, 1983: 57)

Race (English), class (middle) and sex (male) are specified in this hierarchical vision of religious imperialism. 'In Anglican religion the mother is virtually invisible', according to anthropologist Olivia Harris in her essay, 'Heavenly Father'.

Encouraging (manly) ambition in Jane, St John disparages the feminized professions of teacher and clergyman as 'narrow and narrowing ... tranquil, hidden' (356) – too small for their imperialistically large worldly appetites. When he offers her the teaching job he says: 'how poor the proposal is, – how trivial – how cramping.... Knitting, sewing, reading, writing, cyphering, will be all you will have to teach. What will you do with your accomplishments? What, with the largest proportion of your mind – sentiments – tastes?' (356–7). Such flattering recognition of her 'manly' intellect is enough to keep a dutiful daughter running a father's errands for a good many months, and St John's later praise of her success at his mission, telling Mr Oliver 'in strong terms his approbation of what I had done at Morton School' (372), is enough to make her reject Rosamund Oliver's (female) idea for a promotion: 'Indeed! she is clever enough to be a governess in a high family, papa' (372). We need not rehearse again the hidden costs of being a governess (not to mention being a woman) in order to see why Jane stays home earning boy scout badges from her spiritual accountant of a scout master. St John encourages her rising expectations and inadvertantly her feminism, the part of her that knows and values her 'unfeminine' intellect, strength, and energy. For as long as she can grow by his lights, Jane will not quit the troop. But his light is paradoxically very cold, leading Jane to wonder whether St John has a heart underneath 'all his firmness and self-control'. Her yearning is pathetically simple: to be loved as a woman, for her heart, if that's what St John thinks women have to offer; and, more pathetic still, if not to be loved then to be allowed to love, to sympathize with his feelings.

Though he 'locks every feeling and pang within – expresses, confesses, imparts nothing', she does find a way in. Using her pen and perception, Jane is able to 'discover the secret spring of [his] confidence, and find an aperture in that marble breast through which [she] can shed one drop of the balm of sympathy' *(373)*. She draws Rosamund's portrait and then reads St John's reaction to it, and proposes marriage – as a test. St John confirms Rosamund's all-to-feminine deficiencies as a missionary's wife, which Jane had already scathingly summed up for herself when she 'completed Rosamund Oliver's miniature' *(372)* as 'very charming ... but ... not profoundly interesting or thoroughly impressive' *(370)*. Jane's bold move also elicits a complimentary (and unfeminine) portrait of Jane: 'You *are* original,' said he, 'and not timid. There is something brave in your spirit, as well as penetrating in your eye' *(377)*.

Now we are on Jane's territory, where she can speak as freely as she did in proposing to Rochester, without 'the medium of custom, conventionalities, or even of mortal flesh: – it is my spirit that addresses your spirit; just as if ... we stood at God's feet, equal, – as we are!' *(255)*. *Her* power is this welding of emotional, intellectual, and spiritual strength into speech, articulating her claim for equality and direct communication between the sexes. Rather than ignoring or transcending gender, she speaks *as a woman*: as original, brave, and penetrating as reason and feeling can be when working together and not at cross-purposes, as the sex-segregated proprieties of courtship demand.

> Again the surprised expression crossed his face. He had not imagined that a woman would dare to speak so to a man. For me, I felt at home in this sort of discourse. I could never rest in communication with strong, discreet, and refined minds, whether male or female, till I had passed the outworks of conventional reserve, and crossed the threshold of confidence, and won a place by their heart's very hearthstone. *(377)*

Jane may be 'at home' with heart-to-heart communication, but St John is not. He virtually disclaims the existence of his own heart, and disowns any interest in Jane's. He speaks as a convention-bound man, who 'scorns the weakness' of 'feeling' as 'a mere fever of the flesh: not ... the soul. *That* is just as fixed as a rock. ... Know me to be what I am – a cold hard man' *(377)*. He sounds like Charles Kingsley trumpeting the manful and scorning nursemaidism, when he boasts that:

> Reason, and not Feeling, is my guide; my ambition is unlimited;
> my desire to rise higher, to do more than others, insatiable. I
> honour endurance, perseverance, industry, talent; because these
> are the means by which men achieve great ends, and mount to
> lofty eminence. I watch your career with interest, because I
> consider you a specimen of a diligent, orderly, energetic woman:
> not because I deeply compassionate what you have gone
> through, or what you still suffer. (377)

Mounting to the lofty eminence of greatness, there presumably
to get a look at his Father 'in the face, in full assurance of faith
and love', St John insists that Jane travel light if she's going His
way. Compassion in his view is dead weight. As Arnold
Schwarzenegger's sidekick explained about the great man's
stoicism, 'Conan doesn't cry. I cry *for* Conan.' Masculinity as
hyperrationality, and religion as right reason, are the mighty
legs that St John stands on. The epic dimension of St John's
Miltonic stance is only slightly undercut by his computer-nerd
determination that the spirit can be fully accounted for by a
businesslike approach. Because at this point St John's power
over Jane is nearing its zenith, his self-portrait as a great man
she views with considerably more awe than irony.

St John actually gets to play God, not just speak for Him,
when he reads Jane Eyre on a seemingly blank piece of paper,
and puts that clue together with his uncle's legacy and the
advertisements for the missing Jane Eyre. He hands Jane her
identity – name, family (they are cousins), inheritance, and all
that goes with wealth: 'the importance twenty thousand pounds
would give you; the place it would enable you to take in society;
the prospects it would open to you' (389). St John sees the value
of the money, being a very worldly man of the cloth, while
Jane's gratitude is all for the family conferred on her, and the
opportunity to 'indulge [her] feelings' with 'the delicious
pleasure ... of repaying, in part, a mightly obligation, and
winning to myself life-long friends' (289), by dividing up 'the
independence, the affluence' (388) into four parts and reuniting
a family scattered by employment. St John counsels her to follow

custom and law and keep the cash 'with a clear conscience'. 'With me,' said I [Jane], 'it is fully as much a matter of feeling as of conscience' (*389*). When she then asks for St John's brotherly love, she gets his approval instead, grounded in respect for [her] worth, and admiration of [her] talents' (*390*) – praise, from him, but hardly unconditional, and not enough warmth to keep water from freezing in a bucket. Indeed, their newly discovered familial relationship seems to increase his distance. She notes that:

> his reserve was again frozen over, and my frankness was congealed beneath it. He had not kept his promise of treating me like his sisters; he continually made little, chilling, differences between us ... I could hardly comprehend his present frigidity. (*398*)

Jane's identity riddle is solved by St John, only to have another take its place. This one is for Jane to solve for herself, the riddle of her relationship to St John, from the moment when 'I found myself under the influence of the ever-watchful blue eye.' ('The bluest eye' is what the Afro-American writer Toni Morrison features as the Anglo-American God.) 'So keen was it, and so cold, I felt for the moment superstitious – as if I were sitting in the room with something uncanny' (*399*).

The uncanny, that creepy threat of transgression over the boundary of the familiar, the familial, and the proper, haunts Jane's second courtship with the same underground pull that Bertha exerted at Thornfield. Again, what is unacknowledged and unwelcome is both sexual and aggressive, a dark promise of liberation from suffocating circumstances at a forbidding but unknown cost. At Thornfield it was Jane's unarticulated hope that her desires be given full play in courtship, no matter how large, dark, and hairy they might be. She snuffed this hope when she saw how unlovable it proved in the body of Bertha. At Moor House the uncanny is the unarticulated hope of fulfilling equally illegitimate desires, also unrealizable: for the father's love and appreciation of Jane *as a woman*. For his part, St John's hope of lovelessly enthralling Jane is equally uncanny, paradoxical. His 'keen yet cold' domination of Jane provides interest and attachment, but forever witholds love and compassion, to the point of arrogantly commandeering the place of love without providing the feeling. So great is his presumption that his will is God's and duty can be made to fill all hearts with heavenly purpose, that he proposes marriage as a mission he can enlist and train Jane for, the more contrary to her feelings the greater the achievement of subduing them, all 'heathen passions' merely awaiting a parson to school them.

> I am the servant of an infallible master. I am not going out under human guidance, subject to the defective laws and erring control of my feeble fellow-worms: my king, my lawgiver, my captain, is the All-perfect. It seems strange to me that all round me do not burn to enlist under the same banner, – to join in the same enterprise. (*404*)

His unselfconscious identification of himself with God gives his marriage-and-mission proposition uncanny power, in both its attractiveness and repulsiveness to Jane, and its dubiously authorized divinity and sexuality.

When St John turns this unwieldy ambition upon Jane, she recognizes that something 'uncanny' is at work, something unseen lurks behind his request: 'I want you to give up German, and learn Hindostanee' (*399*). Hindostanee? St John is starting to sound like the blind old despot Milton, dutifying his daughters into secretarial slavery to *Paradise Lost*. While he busily rewrote Genesis with more authoritative misogyny, his two daughters read him Greek and Latin they could not understand. Charlotte Brontë in St John borders on satire of the pretensions and exploitations behind such a father's overweening ambition. George Eliot casts the Milton family scene in *Middlemarch* as much at the daughter's expense as the father's – and so reveals her investment, real and idealized, in such a father. Dorothea plays 'good daughter' to Casaubon, who none the less fears her servitude will turn into subversion.

> 'Could I not be preparing myself now to be more useful?' said Dorothea to [Casaubon], one morning, early in the time of

courtship; 'could I not learn to read Latin and Greek aloud to you, as Milton's daughters did to their father, without understanding what they read?'

'I fear that would be wearisome to you,' said Mr Casaubon smiling; 'and, indeed, if I remember rightly, the young women you have mentioned regarded that exercise in unknown tongues as a ground for rebellion against the poet.'

'Yes; but in the first place they were very naughty girls, else they would have been proud to minister to such a father; and in the second place they might have studied privately and taught themselves to understand what they read, and then it would have been interesting. I hope you don't expect me to be naughty and stupid?'

(Gilbert and Gubar, 1979:214)

Dorothea hopes that marrying Casaubon is the key to all knowledge for her, all hope of greatness, and George Eliot confirms that 'it would deliver her from her girlish subjection to her own ignorance, and give her the freedom of voluntary submission to a guide who would take her along the grandest path' (Gilbert and Gubar, 1979:217). Dorothea thinks,

I should learn everything then.... It would be my duty to study that I might help him the better in his great works. There would be nothing trivial about our lives. Everyday things with us would mean the greatest things.... I should learn to see the truth by the same light as great men have seen it by.... I should see how it was possible to lead a grand life here – now – in England.

(Gilbert and Gubar, 1979:215)

Just as Dorothy discovers that the Wizard of Oz is actually a very small man operating the Wizard façade from backstage, Dorothea discovers that Casaubon is rather less than she had idealized as 'Author of The Key to All Mythologies' (his title, not hers). He's a parody of Milton, according to Gilbert and Gubar in *The Madwoman in the Attic*, and as such, I would add, a true son of St John in 'his repudiation of the guilty flesh, his barely disguised contempt for Dorothea's femininity, his tyranny, and his dogmatism' (Gilbert and Gubar, 1979:218).

Picking apart Milton has been great sport for feminists, Charlotte Brontë's Shirley among the first: 'Milton was great;

but was he good? His brain was right; how was his heart?'
(Brontë, 1974:314–15). Distinguishing between greatness and
goodness, intellect and feeling, she breaks Milton down into
gender-specific virtues and finds him wanting, especially in his
understanding of women, Eve in particular: 'Milton tried to see
the first woman; but Cary, he saw her not. . . . It was his cook
that he saw,' Shirley speculates. His epic vision – 'Angels serried
before him their battalions . . . Devils gathered their legions in
his sight' – was blind to woman's epic stature. It's enough to
make the epic itself suspect as the key to all mythologies.

Virginia Woolf, upon reading *Paradise Lost*, tries to analyze
why an epic so 'majestic' can 'let in so little light . . . in judging
life'. Like Jane and Shirley, she see heartlessness as a moral
problem of epic proportions.

> I am struck by the extreme difference between this poem and any
> other. It lies, I think, in the sublime aloofness and impersonality
> of the emotion. . . . The substance of Milton is all made of
> wonderful, beautiful, and masterly descriptions of angels'
> bodies, battles, flights, dwelling places. He deals in horror and
> immensity and squalor and sublimity but never in the passions
> of the human heart. Has any great poem ever let in so little light
> upon one's own joys and sorrows? I get no help in judging life; I
> scarcely feel that Milton lived or knew men and women; . . .
> Moreover, though there is nothing like Lady Macbeth's terror or
> Hamlet's cry, no pity or sympathy or intuition, the figures are
> majestic; in them is summed up much of what men thought of
> our place in the universe, of our duty to God, our religion.
>
> (Gilbert and Gubar, 1979:190)

If as 'much of what men thought of our place in the universe, of
our duty to God, our religion' is as uninformed as *Paradise Lost*
is by any knowledge of the human heart, then Jane's alternative
morality begins to look radical in its difference.

She is not ready to speak her difference to St John or herself,
however, but remains under his spell for reasons she cannot
fathom. The clearer she sees his bullying, the more effectively
she is bullied.

He strips naked the power relations of paternalism and
commands her consent. Jane paradoxically feels his will as both

a salvation ('My work, which had appeared so vague, so hopelessly diffuse, condensed itself as he proceeded, and assumed a definite form under his shaping hand') *and* a death ('My iron shroud contracted round me; persuasion advanced with slow sure step' (*406*)). His version of marriage excludes not only passion but love, even liking; all that is left is duty, with one who 'knew neither mercy nor remorse', who claims Jane 'not for my pleasure, but for my Sovereign's service,' (*405*). What is uncanny is the attractiveness of St John's hideous offer to Jane. What explains the uncanny is the nature of the father-daughter relationship unconsciously structuring St John's and Jane's 'keen yet cold' bond.

It is the fantasy of a father without a wife, and an eldest daughter without a mother or a dowry. Their common religious and intellectual convictions are enough to make such a pair consider a common domestic destiny, one legitimized by duty and propriety, and fed by ambitions vicariously fulfilled. The father's ever-watchful eye on the daughter seeks the measure of his own unfulfilled talents and visions in his daughter's career and prospects, with a 'keen' – desirous – expectation of fulfilment.

Sons stalk their dreams,
Steal their schemes,
Devour their means.
Daughters are a better bet.

(Taylor, 1983b:104)

His needy and resourceful daughter finds her own ambitions enabled by his for her. She learns at his knee that the terms of his ambition for her are the coinage of love in his household. But an attention so keen 'and yet so cold,' so forbidding of desire, makes love uncanny, a contradiction – of promise and want, of approval that somehow seems to preclude love, of family connection that forbids intimacy.

The uncanny vibrates along the lines of the incest taboo, in full harmony with the Victorian ideal of the dutiful daughter. As a little angel in the house serving papa's needs, a girl can show an unselfconscious and socially sanctioned hunger and solicitation for love and approval that would be quite unthinkable outside the family. Charlotte Brontë shows the abjectness of a daughter's need in her novel *Villette*, in Polly's doglike devotion to both her father and future husband. At the same time the impossibility of fulfilling that need, no matter how loyally the daughter follows the father's requirements, fuels the force of the uncanny binding them in mutual expectation. Jane's daughterly resolve is clear: 'By straining to satisfy St John till my sinews ache, I *shall* satisfy him – to the finest central point and farthest outward circle of his expectations' (*407*). She sees that she has won, and can go on winning St John's approval, go on being his special 'study' and 'proving' herself 'by sundry tests' of her 'resolute readiness' to 'perform . . . labour uncongenial to [her] habits and inclinations' (*406*). She can be the dutiful daughter endlessly earning, endlessly yearning.

But: Jane's consciousness-raising 'but' locates her own interests at the crucial moment before self-submergence in the man's. But: his approval does not win her his love, as numerous examples have shown and as St John has himself announced. Jane at last recognizes this fact: 'He will never love me: but he shall approve me' – 'if I *do* make the sacrifice he urges' (*407*). This distinction she makes between love and approval, and her recognition of the conditions upon which his approval rests, is crucial to disentangling herself as a daughter from his paternal power. When she imagines herself as his unloved wife, 'endur[ing] all the forms of love' when 'the spirit was quite absent,' she can find the grounds to reject his proposal: 'No: such a martyrdom would be monstrous' (*407*).

The incest taboo energizes Jane's decisive 'No' and St John's resolute coldness; they each disclaim sexual interest while maintaining the intimacy of shared 'family' ambition. Loving someone 'that way' – physically – incurs a shiver of distaste and fear familiar to pubescent females imaginatively encountering adult sexual relations when still primarily identified with the family as love objects. 'Going all the way', we used to call it in junior high school in 1963, with that thrilling mixture of disbelief and fateful determinism about our own sexual futures that signalled the uncanny. Imagining ourselves was like imagining our parents 'doing it': both transgressed the innocence necessary to our self-definition as women, and the socially sanctioned definition of the family as an innocent place of innocent (non-sexual) desires, within which we were automatically and forever safe, protected *as* our fathers' daughters.

Because the innocence of family and femininity is assumed and socially sanctioned, Jane and St John (and Charlotte Brontë) can easily resist all dirty-minded interpretations of their relationship, its sexual and non-sexual father–daughter aspects alike. No-one, Charlotte Brontë especially, need articulate how essential the father–daughter cathexis is to Jane's struggles into womanhood and feminism, while everyone may participate in Jane's *unconscious* playing out and renegotiation of the dynamic between patriarch and his precocious 'pet' protégée. No-one may accuse Charlotte Brontë of plotting a daughter's mutiny against her father's will, of morally challenging a father who 'does not compassionate' what his daughter suffers as a woman underprotected and overstrained by his ambitions for her. We can still criticize St John's paternalism as such, and reject his marriage proposal to Jane on grounds suggestively similar to incest: because it is loveless and overaggressive in its charges of duty and self-denial, because it violates Jane's integrity and abuses her womanhood.

The sexual aspects are easier to ignore or deny than the aggressive aspects of father–daughter relations because, here, social sanctions approve so much of a father's presumption about the authority of his needs. When St John denies that he *has* any personal needs he wants Jane to fulfil – he'll suppress his *own* passions, thank you very much – he erases the sexual and authorizes (and so hides) the emotional as strictly religious business. His appropriation of Jane's domestic, emotional, spiritual, and intellectual services for his own purposes, he announces, is at once entirely possessive and entirely disinterested: 'A missionary's wife you must – shall be. You shall be mine: I claim you – not for my pleasure, but for my Sovereign's service' (*405*).

Only paternal authority can command a daughter's obedience 'for her own good' with such unselfconscious disclaimers of self-interest, only within a patriarchal religion that authorizes fathers as accountants of their family's spiritual economy. Only the awesome power of the father as conscience itself – 'It was as if I had heard a summons from Heaven' *(404)* – can inspire a daughter's 'wish to please him' to the point where 'I must disown half my nature, stifle half my faculties, wrest my tastes from their original bent, force myself to the adoption of pursuits for which I had no natural vocation' *(401)*. Self-suppression, self-policing, self-censorship, self-denial, originate in Jane's 'impossible' wish to 'mould my irregular features to his correct and classic pattern' *(401)*. How painfully detailed is the process by which her own conscience seems to bully Jane out of her own nature for her own good. She is tempted by 'absolute submission' to St John's every pious prescription for her, his promise that 'I can set your task from hour to hour; stand by you always; help you from moment to moment' *(405)*, as an absolute and given solution to the meaning and spiritual accountability of her life.

Yet finally, it is both the completeness and the coldness of St John's conception of conscience that is to awaken her from 'the freezing spell' of her ambiguously coerced and ambivalently granted consent. As feminist detective, when she looks closely at 'consent' she finds some coercion; when she tests 'cold' objectivity and 'complete' authority and knowledge, she finds some rather warm biases and incomplete, even narrow, perspectives; and when she examines family she finds 'the tyranny that is built into the structure of the family and disguises itself as love' (Marcus, 1984:96).

To the extent to which the character of St John resembles the Reverend Patrick Brontë in his coldness, religiosity, intellectual ambition, and rigid sense of his daughters' duty and loyalty to him, one wonders how Charlotte Brontë may have felt about the losses incurred in the household he ran: the mother who died after bearing six children in seven years, the two eldest daughters who died at the Clergy Daughters School, taken there by a father who approved it enough to send Emily and

Charlotte by return post. The grim conditions described at Lowood in *Jane Eyre* were faithful to her real experience, Charlotte continued to assert, in the face of the storm of critical protest about exaggeration, unfairness, and libel; her anger at the institution's inhumanity and the director's bullying piety pins the blame for the girls' deaths on Lowood's punishingly overconscientious interpretation of humility. Charlotte Brontës's mother, as she lay dying, was beset by religious doubt; the Brontë children as adolescents also passed through crises of spiritual despair and questioning. One does not have to look long at the Reverend's capacity to empathize with the sufferings of the females following his dictates of duty to see some room for doubt about whether he did in fact know their own good or only preached it.

And then there is the killing contrast of the Reverend's expectations for his son – 'My brilliant, unhappy son!' (Peters, 1986:163) – and his daughters: 'Girls,' he said after Charlotte gave him *Jane Eyre* to read, 'do you know Charlotte has been writing a book, and it is much better than likely?' (Peters, 1986: 217). Charlotte explains that when Branwell died (from opium and alcohol addiction and the will to self-destruction as much as anything else):

> My poor father naturally thought more of his *only* son than of his daughters, and, much and long as he had suffered on his account, he cried out for his loss like David for that of Absalom – my son! my son! – and refused at first to be comforted. And then when I ought to have been able to collect my strength and be at hand to support him, I fell ill.
>
> (Peters, 1986:233)

When Emily died three months after Branwell, Charlotte writes (again to her friend and publisher), 'My father and my sister Anne are far from well. . . . My father says to me almost hourly, "Charlotte, you must bear up – I shall sink if you fail me." These words – you can conceive are a stimulus to nature' (Peters, 1986:239). The Reverend endlessly compassionating Branwell's sufferings, supporting his dependencies, and excusing his moral failings, while assuming Charlotte's self-denying services to the family, must have been something of an eye-opener for this endlessly dutiful daughter, who not only played angel in the house but also brought home the bacon as governess, teacher, and writer. Endlessly earning, endlessly yearning.

For Jane Eyre, even as her father, even as her Maker Himself, St John's appropriation of her services becomes *in*appropriate, amounting to a violation of Jane's integrity when it infringes on her self-interest and ability to choose for herself. His domination of her as his subordinate and dependant borders on coercive, she notes with alarm: 'By degrees, he acquired a certain influence over me that took away my liberty of mind' (*400*). It is the nature of his 'influence' as well as the conditions for her 'liberty of mind' that raise questions in Jane's feminist consciousness. Who sets the terms for marital consent? St John-as-pater assumes he structures their relations of inequality. But feminists would counter that a dependant's 'consent' is no longer valid as a ticket to free exploitation written by the powerful. Rather, the nature of St John's moral authority that *assumes* her consent is exactly what Jane is so radically beginning to question. Just as she challenged the structural terms of Rochester's 'mastery' of their moral relations, Jane challenges St John's 'ascendancy' in their relations. His idea of marriage is strictly patriarchal, at least one generation out-of-date: a 'permanent conformity' of interests, the wife goose-stepping as 'sole helpmeet' to the husband as dictator, 'fitted to [his] purpose', his 'influence' and 'absolute retention until death' (*408*).

Jane's objection comes as a Dissenter's claim for the priority of individual conscience, which not coincidentally grants the woman (as wife or daughter) the right, not just to refusal, but to an alternative morality challenging the absoluteness of His word. Jane's resistance to St John is more than just a 'No' to a grim marriage: it is an answer to every prescription for her spiritual salvation that he has defined for her.

Jane is too proud, and too systematic and ambitious an analyst to leave the matter at a simple rejection of him, his undue influence, his overbearingness, his stingy marriage offer.

'It's nothing *personal*,' St John says in perhaps one of the most flattening marriage proposals ever. In rejecting him, Jane offers a critique of his ideas and authority that is likewise not so much personal as a wholesale assault on his world view.

When she says she'll 'give the missionary my energies – it is all he wants – but not myself' *(408–9)*, she challenges his authority over her as well as his loveless terms of possession. When St John answers that 'I cannot accept on His behalf a divided allegiance: it must be entire' *(409)*, he cowardly hides his claim behind God's, while brazenly speaking for Him, a sleight-of-hand that Jane immediately deconstructs by distinguishing between him and God:

> 'Oh! I will give my heart to God,' I said. '*You* do not want it.'
>
> I will not swear, reader, that there was not something of repressed sarcasm both in the tone in which I uttered this sentence, and in the feeling that accompanied it. I had silently feared St John till now, because I had not understood him. He had held me in awe, because he had held me in doubt. How much of him was saint, how much mortal, I could not heretofore tell: but revelations were being made in this conference: the analysis of his nature was proceeding before my eyes. I saw his fallibilities: I comprehended them. I understood that ... I sat at the feet of a man, erring as I. The veil fell from his hardness and despotism. Having felt in him the presence of these qualities, I felt his imperfection, and took courage. I was with an equal – one with whom I might argue – one whom, if I saw good, I might resist.
>
> He was silent after I had uttered the last sentence, and I presently risked an upward glance at his countenance. His eye, bent on me, expressed at once stern surprise and keen inquiry 'Is she sarcastic, and sarcastic to *me*!' it seemed to say.
>
> 'What does this signify?' *(409)*

A daughter demystifying a father's godlike authority notices with just such sarcasm his feet of clay. Angry and confused as to who should feel more humiliated at the revelation, she is yet emboldened by his incomprehension (a sudden blindness) and her own certainty about her change in perception (a sudden sight).

The power of this moment is in Jane's dispelling of the

uncanny by solving the riddle of their power relation. It is a confrontation with a paternal authority so great that he held Jane's destiny in his hands, the judgment of her intellect and spirit, and the means of her material and social livelihood. St John has appeared to her as the door – to education, work, family, ladyhood, legacy, self-respect, and spiritual salvation – Heaven itself. Realistically, he was, that's the sad truth, but also Jane's *enabling* truth. His godlike mystery and her awe blinded her to the mortal limits of their pact's power. When the veil fell she saw, behind the curtain of the Wizard of Oz, only 'a man' and therefore 'an equal'. The sequence of demystification is the very process of feminist analysis and empowerment: 'Revelations' follow on her 'analysis', 'comprehension' drops the veil from mystified authority and presents her with a being as imperfect as herself, whose equality authorizes her own voice. Blindness yields to sight, awe yields to sympathetic understanding, silent fear yields to the courage to speak and to conscientiously resist. Jane's vision and conclusion are the crucial step from dependence and victimhood, from the received idea of dutiful daughterhood as achieved femininity, to an assertive vision of womanhood that locates her own power, not just in resistance but in alternative vision and initiative. 'Faced by the quality of male authority and by the unreliability of many of the men who wield it', a heroine learns 'to find in the interstices of that authority the exact extent of her own possibilities for individual initiative', as Jane Miller explains this feminist process (Miller, 1986:59).

Jane combats religious certainty with romantic revelation. Having seen through a glass darkly, she authorizes her own vision to see Him face to face. Forsaking Milton's Eve's place ('he for God, she for God in him'), she steps into her own place for her own Eve, 'just as if . . . we stood at God's feet, equal, – as we are!' (*255*). Eve in Shirley's vision is 'heaven born' with 'the daring which could contend with Omnipotence: face to face she speaks with God' (Brontë, 1974:315–16). She resembles Jane's moon mother and portrait of the Evening Star.

It is both as a daughter and potential wife that Jane resists St John's oppressive version of marriage. Both daughter-as-career and wife-as-career to such a patriarch require 'absolute submission': '"A part of me you must become," he answered steadily; "otherwise the whole bargain is void"' (*410*). Adam's Rib makes a very stunted angel in St John's house:

> as his wife – at his side always, and always restrained, and always checked – forced to keep the fire of my nature continually low, to compel it to burn inwardly and never utter a cry, though the imprisoned flame consumed vital after vital – *this* would be unendurable. (*410*)

He grants her no right to privacy, to difference, to her own heart and mind, or body: no habeas corpus clause in King John's 'unMagnanimous Charta'. His is a 'killing' marriage: 'I felt how – if I were his wife, this good man, pure as the deep sunless source, could soon kill me: without drawing from my veins a single drop of blood, or receiving on his own crystal conscience the faintest stain of crime' (*413–14*). This charge, of St John's murderous results, if not motives, makes sainthood and angelhood look more like death and entombment than lifegiving salvation: the sunless and bloodless purity of ice, drained of all life, all feeling.

St John responds to Jane's challenge of his authority and his offer, not with a change in his perception or feeling, but with more of the same, with an Arctic blast of his usual servings of frozen reserve, frigidity, and freezing spell. Jane sees from her new perspective the hostility and vengeance seething under St John's will to dominate. 'As a man, he would have wished to coerce me into obedience' (*412*). His coldness is not the objective disinterest of God's own businessman, accountable only to 'the facts, Ma'am, just the facts'. His coldness is a great frozen continent of anger, breaking open with disappointment.

> Reader, do you know, as I do, what terror those cold people can put into the ice of their questions? How much of the fall of the avalanche is in their anger? of the breaking up of the frozen sea in their displeasure? (*415*)

By telling him this she brings the avalanche crashing down on her head. She breaks the spell of the uncanny *by speaking* the unspeakable and uncovering the hidden, the aggression and coercion of St John's will:

> '... you almost hate me. If I were to marry you, you would kill me. You are killing me now.'
>   His lips and cheeks turned white – quite white.
>   '*I should kill you – I am killing you?* Your words are such as ought not to be used: violent, unfeminine, and untrue.' (*415*)

Significantly, St John challenges her on her *words*, recognizing that they have already had the power to disenthrall Jane and to undermine his authority. He identifies but cannot counter her verbal violence of opposition, because 'these words ... touched on the truth' (*415*) of St John's power *and its limits*. In particular, it's the lovelessness of his morality that Jane finds to be the 'Freon in his icebox'. On this point she rejects him, as her conscience, mate, and father-knows-best at once:

> 'I scorn your idea of love,' I could not help saying; as I rose up and stood before him, leaning my back against the rock. 'I scorn the counterfeit sentiment you offer: yes, St John, and I scorn you when you offer it.' (*411*)

There's a symmetry to Jane's moral stands at Thornfield and Moor House. Jane scorned Rochester's idea of love too, remember, his counterfeit marriage offer of all passion and no security. St John is all security guard and no love, equally unacceptable as a serious marriage proposal. But there's a difference that even St John's gentleness cannot obscure from Jane's beady little eye: 'he surrounded me with his arms, *almost* as if he loved me (I say *almost* – I knew the difference – for I had felt what it was to be loved ...)' (*422*). Before true love sounds its trumpet call and the hand of fate whisks Jane away to find her man, before she hears Rochester call, '"Jane! Jane! Jane!" nothing more' (*422*), and snatches feminist victory from the jaws of feminine defeat, let us pause to examine the power of love here, so lacking in St John and so telepathically present in Rochester.

First, let me distinguish love from true love. True love in the reductiveness of romantic fiction is the *deus ex machina* of lovers' hearts and plots, an absolute, an essence governing but hardly explaining both feeling and reason; true love is a substitute for real human motivation in all its embarrassing ambiguities and less-than-honorable intentions. Love, on the other hand, as Charlotte Brontë represents it in her novel, is the capacity to understand as much as to feel, to stand firm as much as to compromise, and to receive with as much gain as to give.

Love, then, enables Rochester to see Jane in all her mighty oppositions and less-than-fully-feminine attractions, especially after she at last stands up to him and unmasks his more oppressive ideas about women and her own radical alternatives. Love enables Rochester to counter his own interests with Jane's, and to search for the common moral ground that does violence to neither one's integrity. St John's inability to break out of his own egotism – to love – condemns him to a blindness to others' interests and perspectives that results in a crippling incapacity to feel, 'compassionate suffering', even to recognize his own. 'The want of sympathy condemns us to a corresponding stupidity' is George Eliot's formulation of this moral limitation.

The blinded and stumbling, one-handed former patriarch leaning on Jane in the end is the *smart* guy, the one who can read the legitimate limits of his power over others, and rewrite his ending in terms morally acceptable to – accepting of – Jane and her vision. The arrogantly envisioned, two-fisted, aspiring superpatriarch, who won't acknowledge that he leans on everyone to prove his own autonomy, is the man unfit for marriage because he is incapable of the moral transformation that marriage entails in Jane's – and every woman's – ever-so-capable hands.

Chapter Four

FROM BAD GIRL TO GOOD WOMAN

W HEN I draw up the curtain the last time, dear reader, imagine yourself on the outskirts of a typical Victorian family, dear dead Papa, alternately scolding and spoiling Mama, big-bosomed and heavily draped, three whining overgrown children already rendered socially useless by a domestic education overinvested in gentility and underinvested in morality. Imagine the witness to this family as a 'precocious outcast' ready to 'act out' her critique with a vengeance. And hear the singularly authoritative voice of the narrator, directing our attention first to this ten-year-old's predicament, and now to the scene within Jane, her secret thoughts and dreams. There is something very private and very public about this story being shown as much as told first-hand. A play!

Jane's rebellious acts of self-definition can be viewed as Scene One of her autobiography-as-performance. She steps out from behind the red moreen curtains and repeats her lines in obedience to John Reed's familiar bullying script. When he hits her with her book she strikes back with improvisation, name-calling gleaned from a script of her own reading, Goldsmith's *History of Rome*. Her tantrum garners an excited audience of the whole household. Their reactions further her process of self-definition-through-audience-provocation. By calling her 'a fury', 'a mad cat' and 'a picture of passion', Bessie and Abbot pinpoint her social problem: passion and its physicality are strictly forbidden by the code of femininity-as-gentility that rules the Reed household. By dramatizing herself as the heroine of her own production, finding inspiration for her improvisatory scripts in books, her antagonists in all the unfair expectations inflicted on her, and her audience in the household itself, Jane enacts her exciting story of self-creation using the scripts and props and cast of all-too-ordinary life itself.

Who is the audience for Jane Eyre's fiery opening act? Who is the reader later addressed by the narrator? Who are those critics who 'blame' Jane Eyre for her discontent on Thornfield's battlements? Always, the three productions and producers stand one behind the other – heroine, narrator/autobiographer, novelist – and while each does implicitly address her own audience, each must pretend there is no public audience, no actress, no performance at all. 'Entangled in notions of feminine propriety' (Stoneman, 1987:177), a lady – a ten-year-old girl, a matron, a single-woman writer – does not perform or speak in public. Yet 'Speak I *must*: I had been trodden on severely, and *must* turn: but how?' (*38*). Charlotte Brontë's solution is a threefold 'cover', disguising Jane Eyre's public debate of the woman question as a memoir, one woman's story of her private pilgrimage from bad girl to good woman.

Jane Eyre's threefold cover, very like a curtain on a stage, at once announces and hides the public nature of the performance. As audience, we pretend we're not there, as long as the performers pretend we're invisible; real life is in their hands, not ours, as we watch. Any coy peeks from behind the red moreen curtains, however, can disturb our willing suspension of disbelief. We can see that we in the audience are not invisible or incidental, but the point of the production, its *raison d'être*. Three peeks at the audience reveal each of *Jane Eyre*'s three hidden actresses – the character, the narrator, and the novelist.

First, Jane Eyre as a young woman explains that she must act like a lady in order to persuade others of her respectability. Her audience in effect determines her role. From the first moment of her career as a single woman, when she launches herself from the convent of Lowood without social connection or chaperonage, Jane Eyre must protect her own reputation with an eagle-eye on propriety. 'A private fear ... haunted me,' she tells us, 'that in thus acting for myself, and by my own guidance, I ran the risk of getting into some scrape; and, above all things, I wished the result of my endeavours to be respectable, proper, *en règle*' (*91*). She must always be aware of her audience, of how she is seen. Her acute self-consciousness points to her new vulnerability as an unprotected object of public attention and moral categorization. To be seen as a lady is Jane's sole self-protection. Reputation is her life-raft, kept afloat by her audience's approval.

The narrator then likens this moment in her life, when she is first on her own in public, to a new scene in a play. 'And when I draw up the curtain this time, reader, you must fancy you see a [private] room in the George Inn at Millcote' where 'I sit in my cloak and bonnet ... waiting, while all sorts of doubts and fears are troubling my thoughts' (*96*). The reader is assigned the role of a member of the audience at a play, the narrator steps out from behind the red moreen curtain and announces that she is the director and producer, and that Jane is an actress exposed to our scrutiny. Rather than the privacy and solitude of the acts of novel reading, novel writing, and autobiographical self-revelation, suddenly we are all of us publicly exposed in our places as watcher, director, and actress. The realization that we are not hiding or alone, but *seen and categorized by what we are doing*, is a shock of the kind Jane Eyre experienced when she was first exposed to the world's eyes as a woman.

How might one feel about such a suddenly precarious and victimized moral position as a woman, subject to the vision and conclusions of others, especially after years of moral education and growing confidence in one's own abilities and judgment as a woman of intellect and spirit? The single woman emerges from her single-sex education and finds, to her disbelief, that all her work and most of her self are invisible; she is seen only as a woman, any woman, every woman, and subjected to the only test: is she womanly enough? From an active agent in her own journey, she is reduced to passivity, to waiting on others' ideas about her social self. The overwhelming frustration and fear of such a moment, when a woman is reduced to defending her womanhood to strangers, and her very survival depends upon her recognizing and responding to the terms on which she is being judged, is a familiar yet unspoken part of every woman's life, particularly at adolescence when her body comes into focus in the public eye as provocation and prey. At worst, her self-protective conformity to propriety can feel like self-betrayal, and the expectations of others like an invisible assault on her integrity. At best, such a moment can make clear that since femininity is indeed a socially created role, quite dependent on the audience assessment, *audience can be addressed* about the terms of evaluation.

'Who blames me?' Jane demands from Thornfield's battlements. 'Many, no doubt; and I shall be called discontented' (*112*). Charlotte Brontë here addresses her critics on her heroine's moral qualifications as heroine. The nature and duties of Jane Eyre as a woman are the issue, and the novelist Charlotte Brontë takes issue with public moralists on the woman question, with a certainty that she and her heroine will be blamed. And blamed they were for challenging convention.

'Conventionality is not morality. Self-righteousness is not religion. To attack the first is not to assail the last' (*v–vi*). Charlotte Brontë in the preface to the second edition of *Jane Eyre* addresses her critics sharply because they missed her point. She scolds those who called Jane immoral or amoral. Jane Eyre's morality in its unconventionality is no less – indeed is more – sincerely religious than the cant that passes for morality among the self-righteous and genteel. That's the whole point of the Gateshead chapters, for God's sake: can't her intended audience read themselves in Mrs Reed, John Reed, and Mr Brocklehurst?

Jane Eyre's invisible audience contests her control over her life and story, from the very nature of Jane as a ten-year-old girl, to the propriety of exposing her tantrum, and justifying her rebellion, to a very public audience: the Victorian middle class. By simultaneously addressing and ignoring her audience of contemporaries, Charlotte Brontë engages in public debate under the cover of a private woman telling a fireside tale to her own family.

Charlotte Brontë's cleverest conjuring trick is to use the genteel pretence of autobiography. Ostensibly, it is one lady's private confession, written as an overlong letter to a friend, addressed intimately as her dear reader. As Pamela's letters literally form the content of Samuel Richardson's novel *Pamela*, Jane's scenes form the content of her narration. Autobiography authorizes the narrator's feminine innocence and purity of motive and behaviour by casting her as a lady happily hidden within the household, quietly penning her memoirs. Yet the fact is that the Reed household and the heroine's own interior, both disordered by Jane's temper tantrum and reconstituted by her self-control, are exposed to public scrutiny by readers much more like the audience at a play. The doll's house is opened and peered into by all: *the novel makes domestic surveillance a matter for public debate.* Jane Eyre *is* 'an underhand little thing,' as accused and convicted, 'with so much cover,' for spying on the Reeds as 'an uncongenial alien in their midst,' and then exposing their family secret: the moral hypocrisy at the heart of a materialistic gentility.

Jane's audience is the middle class itself, especially its public moralists. By swivelling to take a look out at the audience for Jane Eyre's performance – Charlotte Brontë's contemporaries, quarrelling noisily amongst themselves about the nature, behaviour, duties and rights of the woman on stage as historical actress – we can see Jane Eyre's redefinition project in its ambitiously aimed context, the terms of middle-class morality itself. Mrs Reed, as head of the Gateshead household, is her first target.

GATESHEAD: WOMAN'S INFLUENCE

The particular target of Jane's satire is Mrs Reed's mothering, her spoiling her own children by ignoring or defending their faults, and her punishing Jane with 'stern, relentless' exclusion

(*232*). The happy family that is our earliest view of the Reeds is tinged with Jane's sarcasm:

> The said Eliza, John, and Georgiana were now clustered round their mama in the drawing-room: she lay reclined on a sofa by the fireside, and with her darlings about her (for the time neither quarrelling nor crying) looked perfectly happy. Me, she had dispensed from joining the group; saying, 'She regretted to be under the necessity of keeping me at a distance; but that until she heard from Bessie, and could discover by her own observation that I was endeavouring in good earnest to acquire a more sociable and childlike disposition, a more attractive and sprightly manner, – something lighter, franker, more natural as it were – she really must exclude me from privileges intended only for contented, happy, little children.'
> 'What does Bessie say I have done?' I asked.
> 'Jane, I don't like cavillers or questioners: besides, there is something truly forbidding in a child taking up her elders in that manner. Be seated somewhere; and until you can speak pleasantly, remain silent.' (*9*)

Such a portrait of fireside family harmony literally illustrated Mrs. Ellis's advicebooks addressed to the Women, Wives and Daughters of England in the 1840s. It is a picture of childhood innocence and maternal influence as natural emanations, glowing essences like the fire itself. Jane caricatures such a preposterous ideal by showing the real nature of each Reed to be selfish, deceitful, and spiteful.

Jane's satirical view of Mrs Reed has some credibility when Jane is aged ten, angry and alienated, much more when she is aged eighteen and a self-governing governess, with 'firmer trust in myself and my own powers, and less withering dread of oppression. The gaping wound of my wrongs, too, was now quite healed; and the flame of resentment extinguished' (*230*). The portrait Jane draws of Mrs Reed as she is dying is firm and final, a withering indictment of a mother's utter failure of 'influence' in raising her children. Framed by Jane's early experience of Mrs Reed's dependence upon propriety for her rules of conduct, and Jane's successful moral education at Lowood, the Reed family portrait she draws eight years later is all too pointedly contrasted with Jane's self-portrait showing her independence from the 'pride and folly' governing Gateshead's family. While Jane is a successful career woman, her cousins have 'altered past recognition' (*230*) – and not for the better. 'John Reed is dead ... he ruined himself and half-ruined his family' by gambling and threatening his mother with his own death or hers, 'and is supposed to have committed suicide', Jane reports. 'The news so shocked his mother that it brought on an apopletic attack' (*225–6*). Eliza is a religious fanatic of anorectic proportions, and Georgiana a spiteful society creature trying to sell herself on the marriage market as her value drops precipitously with each unsuccessful season. Mrs Reed dies hating and hateful, in Jane's all-forgiving care. The road to the Reed family ruin commenced with Mrs Reed's broken promise to raise Jane as one of her own children, and with fairytale formality, Jane returns to gloat over her former persecutor's demise.

Two fictions of womanhood make hypocrites of Mrs Ellis and Mrs Reed, in Jane's book. Assuming innocence in children and influence in mothers breeds disaster. Real moral education cannot proceed from the deceits inherent in maintaining the facade of 'innocence', or from the powerlessness inherent in 'influence' – a vague maternal instinct towards gentility-as-goodness. Jane as governess sneers at 'solemn doctrines about the angelic nature of children, and the duty of those charged with their education to conceive for them an idolatrous devotion' (*111*).

Mrs Ellis claimed that the middle class was 'the pillar of our nation's strength', and women were the key to that strength through their 'influence'. As Davidoff and Hall (1987) explain in their landmark study, *Family Fortunes*:

> Her advice books and novels assume a world in which the domestic sphere is occupied by women, children and servants, with men as the absent presence. ... Women had both the time, the moral capacity and the influence to exercise real power in the domestic world. It was their responsibility to recreate society from below .... *Influence* was the secret of women's power and that influence, as wives and mothers, meant that they did not need to seek other kinds of legitimation.
>
> (Davidoff and Hall, 1987:181, 183)

The nature of woman's influence was in contention in Charlotte Brontë's day. Mrs Ellis represented the shift away from an earlier evangelical emphasis on salvation, to a secular, class-based emphasis on propriety. 'By the 1840s good taste, the capacity not to be vulgar, was replacing salvation' as the mark of middle-class gentility, according to Davidoff and Hall. 'To be large, or loud, or strong, was to be ugly and carried with it notions of moral collapse as well as physical failure to conform' (Davidoff and Hall, 1987:191).

Gentility-as-goodness, an enduring legacy, relies heavily on dress and etiquette for its rules, as a kind of 'barrier which Society draws round itself, a shield against the intrusion of the impertinent, the improper, and the vulgar', as Mrs Ellis explains (Tannahill, 1982:351). Mrs Reed enforces this barrier of propriety by shielding her own 'good' children from Jane's impertinence, and later punishing Jane's violence with imprisonment, to enforce on her that 'condition of perfect submission and stillness' (20) that represents virtue in her book. Mother and daughter battle for control over the daughter's body/because 'A woman's virtuosity lay in her containment, like a plant in the pot,' as Davidoff and Hall (1987) develop the flower-of-femininity-under-cultivation metaphor. After a kicking-andscreaming rebellion and removal and imprisonment, Jane returns to the drawing room chastened. 'The woman's body was brought back to the centre of femininity' by writers like Mrs Ellis, as Davidoff and Hall (1987:191) explains, 'but it was the body of the contained and domesticated woman'.

Cultivating the female body – appearance, manners self-improvement disciplines – was the curriculum at Gateshead, while cultivating the female mind, and renouncing the body, was the content of Jane's education at Lowood. Eliza is a graduate of the school of female ascetic self-denial, with a PhD in meanness of spirit that makes a mockery of Mrs Ellis's dictum that selflessness is the key to a woman's moral influence. Georgiana struggles to get her second-rate degree in female self-display, eventually awarded by her marriage to a 'wealthy worn-out man of fashion' (244). The two sisters exemplify the worst extremes of cultivating the body to be the female self.

They reveal, as does their mother as she dies, the moral vacuum at the centre of conventional notions of female propriety.

Mrs Ellis's idea of influence lay in a woman's self-renunciation for the family – as if her self, if present, could not be trusted to serve the welfare of others:

> It is necessary for her to lay aside all her natural caprice, her love of self-indulgence, her vanity, her indolence – in short, her very *self* – and assuming a new nature, which [is] to spend her mental and moral capabilities in devising means for promoting the happiness of others, while her own derives a remote and secondary existence from theirs.
>
> (Newton, 1981:5)

Jane Eyre's critique of such a monstrosity of motherhood remains useful to us today. 'Influence' as *only* the power of self-denial-by-example invites martyrdom at best, family ruin at worst, because it involves no real moral education, spiritual inspiration, or empowerment. Mrs Reed collapses weakly in the face of her son's bullying and control of the estate. Property (her son) wins over propriety (her only power) when no spirit (Jane's power) backs her up. Georgiana and Eliza implode as moral vacuums.

Power! Women need real power, such as Jane gains: education, work, equal inheritance with men, and equality within the household. Gateshead shows the failures of Mrs Ellis's type of influence, and Jane moves on to the modern and progressive Lowood, where knowledge from beyond the home provides the grounding for true moral influence.

LOWOOD: THE POWER OF WOMEN'S EDUCATION

Lowood and Miss Temple are the making of Jane Eyre: her education, the food for her soul, the means of her livelihood, and the key to Rochester's attraction to her. What is a 'good education' for a young woman? What is its goal? And who are her best teachers?

Brocklehurst assures Mrs Reed that he has 'studied how best to mortify in them the worldly sentiment of pride' *(36)*. His institution, like a prison, materially structured to enforce humility as the girls' appropriate posture as orphans, objects of charity, and dependants outside the family. He denies them any femininity, especially any curls; ill-suited brown dresses 'gave an air of oddity even to the prettiest' *(49)*, hinting at their odd-woman's fate, the 'third sex' of governesses (Peterson, 1972: 211). His evangelical 'mission is to mortify in these girls the lusts of the flesh; to teach them to clothe themselves with shame-facedness and sobriety, not with braided hair and costly apparel' *(67)*. His wife and daughters show up elaborately coiffed and clothed, and Jane's childish appetite for hypocrisy is gorged by the sight. Sarcasm is her puny weapon, as when she describes grace after a burnt meal as 'thanks being returned for what we had not got' *(48)*. But Miss Temple and Helen Burns show her much more effective ways to subvert Brocklehurst and his mission than the 'unavailing and impotent anger' of 'but a little untaught girl'. Jane is 'weak and silly to say [she] *cannot bear*' injustice, and to say we 'should strike back again very hard ... so hard as to teach the person who struck us never to do it again' *(56–60)*. Jane's style of victory, over Mrs Reed, had left her 'alone, winner of the field', with the bitter poison of vengeance as aftertaste.

Jane learns from the women at Lowood that self-control is the true victory, and must be self-taught. Such discipline cannot be learned by command, force, or public humiliation – all Mr Brocklehurst's powers. Though he starves and freezes and beats and sickens and preaches and bores and threatens the girls with sudden deaths and punishments, he remains quite impotent over the eighty young women because he cannot actually teach. Like his fellow evangelical St John Rivers, he neither loves nor is loved, as Helen Burns tells Jane, and Jane later learns about St John: 'Mr Brocklehurst is not a god: nor is he even a great and admired man: he is little liked here; he never took steps to make himself liked' *(71)*. Power, authority: where do they come from at Lowood? Who controls the female interior?

Jane fears that Brocklehurst is God Himself, that he 'was to brand me as a bad child forever' *(64)*. He certainly gives it his best shot, but he finds himself up against the great marble face of Miss Temple. 'By what authority?' *(65)* does she order more food, offer what he has forbidden, and let curls grow, he publicly thunders at her. 'I must be responsible for the circumstance, sir' *(65)*, she says, and tries 'to smooth away the involuntary smile' *(66)* that shows her secret female power of mind over matter. 'The inside', Jane notes, 'was further beyond his interference than he imagined' *(67)*. Let the learning begin; Jane has found the source of female power, the beloved authority for education.

When Miss Temple brings Jane and Helen to her room and feeds them, Jane's 'grievous load' of fear and resentment and stoicism is lifted, and when Miss Temple publicly vindicates her, 'I from that hour set to work afresh, resolved to pioneer my way through every difficulty: I toiled hard, and my success was proportionate to my efforts' *(77)*. O brave new world, that has such people in it! Jane's dream-come-true sounds like that of M. Carey Thomas in founding Bryn Mawr College in 1872: 'There we would live loving each other and urging each other on to every high and noble deed or action and all who passed should say "their example arouses me, their books ennoble me, their ideas inspire me and behold they are women!" '(Horowitz, 1984:112).

Miss Temple aside from being perfect, knows how to feed the hungry bee, with a fire, food, conversation, tenderness, and vindication. Jane in her presence finds that by moderating and disciplining herself, telling her life story with new reflection, restraint, and coherence, 'it sounded more credible: I felt as I went on that Miss Temple fully believed me' *(73)*. Jane has found a mother, who takes up her case against Brocklehurst and publicly proclaims Jane a good, not a bad girl. She and Helen have found fit food for their 'famished appetites': the knowledgeable conversation of educated women. Wordsworth's 'life of the soul' is incarnated in Miss Temple who offers his three essential foods: admiration, hope, and love (Houghton, 1957:306). Miss Temple remains serene and awesome, a shrine to refined propriety. But Helen Burns takes fire, the inspiration

97

of Romantics racier than Wordsworth, and Jane takes notes:

> The refreshing meal, the brilliant fire, the presence and kind-
> ness of her beloved instructress, or, perhaps, more than all these,
> something in her own unique mind, had roused her powers
> within her. They woke, they kindled: first, they glowed in the
> bright tint of her cheek, which till this hour I had never seen but
> pale and bloodless; then they shone in the liquid lustre of her
> eyes, which had suddenly acquired a beauty more singular than
> that of Miss Temple's – a beauty neither of fine colour nor long
> eyelash, nor pencilled brow, but of meaning, of movement, of
> radiance. Then her soul sat on her lips, and language flowed,
> from what source I cannot tell: has a girl of fourteen a heart large
> enough, vigorous enough to hold the swelling spring of pure,
> full, fervid eloquence?...
>   They conversed of things I had never heard of! of nations and
> times past; of countries far away: of secrets of nature discovered
> or guessed at: they spoke of books: how many they had read!
> What stores of knowledge they possessed! Then they seemed so
> familiar with French names and French authors: but my
> amazement reached its climax when Miss Temple asked Helen if
> she sometimes snatched a moment to recall the Latin her father
> had taught her, and taking a book from a shelf, bade her read
> and construe a page of 'Virgil'; and Helen obeyed, my organ of
> Veneration expanding at every sounding line. (75–6)

Jane's 'organ of Veneration' focuses on Helen's beauty 'of
meaning, of movement, of radiance. Then her soul sat on her
lips, and language flowed....' This is a power worth learning,
an authority generated from making meaning, rather than
having it imposed or memorized. Inspired, Jane takes fire: 'I
learned the first two tenses of the verb *Etre*, and sketched my
first cottage ... on the same day.' That night, instead of
dreaming up delicious meals:

> I feasted instead on the spectacle of ideal drawings, which I saw
> in the dark; all the work of my own hands. ... I would not now
> have changed Lowood with all its privations, for Gateshead and
> its daily luxuries. (77).

Appetite and feeding remain today at the heart of female
adolescence, when the demands of feminine self-denial can be
compensated for by the pleasures of learning as self-feeding.

Jane resolves to locate the verb 'to be' – her own agency – in her education, where the luxury of liberated mind has victory over the privations of mere physical matter. She sketches her first cottage: her first house she can call her own, her own social place as an educated woman.

The sampler over the schoolhouse door might read 'Mind over matter,' with that militant cheerfulness that only half covers the enormity of the loss of the physical. 'I Can Do Without It' (Davidoff and Hall, 1987:414), Jane Taylor's didactic tale (1845) of a fourteen-year-old girl's quandary about how to spend her first dress allowance – not, she decides, on a fancy hat! – captures that moment at which self-display is subordinated to self-improvement, the crux of the educated middle-class woman's identity. Gender identification here gets sacrificed or at least subordinated to class identification as the only way forward. The message is that education cultivates the 'genderless' mind and creates gender equality through women's mental self-improvement. As Mary Wollstonecraft argued in 1792, silly, lightweight, gender behaviour (only girls have gender), clothes-conscious and giggling with coy deference to male attention, is rendered girlishly trivial by the weight of mind in the morality of the middle-class. Jane graduates from Lowood with this lesson well learnt, and goes on to apply it at Thornfield: self-control is the key to self-improvement, which is the key to the equitable household. Jane's power *as governess* is the secret of her success.

THORNFIELD: ROMANCE AND ROMANTICS REVISED

'You are –', Rochester says by way of introduction. 'I am the governess', Jane announces. She will do him good some day, Rochester recognizes at once. Their love at first sight is actually male need and female service recognizing and embracing the gender-interaction that fits them for life. 'It is time some one undertook to rehumanise you' (*439*), Jane says as Mrs Rochester at Ferndean. But by then her work is done.

Pamela's aristocrat, Mr B, explains the problem: 'We people

of fortune, or such as are born to large expectations, of both sexes, are generally educated wrong ... We are so headstrong, so violent in our wills, that we very little bear control' (Armstrong, 1987:129). Rochester and Adèle prove educable by the governess, Blanche and Bertha quite recalcitrant, but all are useful resources for Jane's self-education project.

Thornfield is a stage for Jane, where gothic and Romantic players and scripts are dusted off and scenes enacted for Jane's puritanical scrutiny and prurient enjoyment. Jane is not unlike a Victorian audience watching a Restoration drama, or reading a racy French novel by George Sand, or scanning the gossip columns about Byron's latest escapades on the continent. From her windowseat vantagepoint as governess, Jane 'could see without being seen' and evaluate 'the vulgar herd' of the gentry. Using that dissipated and showy class as counterpoint to her own depth and self-control, Jane finds plenty of evidence for the moral superiority of the protestant ethic embodied in prim governesses such as herself. Blanche is Jane's favourite target, and her moralizing 'portrait of an accomplished lady of rank' pinpoints pride as the cause of her all-too-predictable fall. Blanche exuberantly plays the advicebook stereotype, the Haughty Dame, with all her Quality Airs about her' (Armstrong, 1987:72). Bertha's fall from her high horse happened long ago. This Dark Lady of tropical appetites overfermented in one of the Empire's racier burning climes. And Adèle, quite the actress already, plays 'the little Parisienne' courtesan who dances and sings for applause and gifts.

These colourful characters, along with Rochester's romantic tales of his Byronic escapades, provide Jane with more than enough material not only for class warfare, but also for her own psychic warfare. She proves herself a desirable woman in Rochester's eyes by contrasting herself with the familiar objects of desire for the romantic rake – the lady of rank, the courtesan, and the Empire's exotic Other. She fashions herself *beloved woman as governess*, and makes her class identity into the material of her own psychic self-regulation, by playing Grace Poole to her id's Bertha, governess to Blanche's spoiled Queen, Quaker nun to French coquette – all to Rochester's amusement, appreciation, and applause.

Why does Jane Eyre not fall in love with a middle-class man, a clergyman like St John, or perhaps a mill owner like Rosamund's father? Obviously, they're already domesticated by the protestant ethic, so there's no reformation for Jane to effect, no wifely role worthy of her talents. More important, only at Thornfield does passion play porno-films of sex-as-adventures-in-foreign-capitals. 'Worldliness' means a large map for passion's playground. Thornfield manor's extensive library, attic, parlour, and garden have in them *all the romance and passion ever written into a woman's character and life.* So even while Jane is primly differentiating her *behaviour* from Blanche's and Bertha's, she is boldly portraying her nature with 'full as much soul, and full as much heart'. The 456-page challenge of bringing her fervent mind and body under the reign of reason is due to writing such romantic passion *into* 'woman's nature', and then domesticating them without denying their legitimacy.

To read Thornfield *as* Jane Eyre, her own household for romance, turns its occupants into her own 'gigantic propensities' in gothic plots. She has had a tropical adolescence in Jamaica, all her appetites steaming sweatily in 'the burning clime'. (Charlotte Brontë called her own adolescent fictional world 'the burning clime' and renounced it at the age of twenty-two, when the world of work and duty called.) Rochester is her chance at a European gent's education in love, money, and power among the jet set, and then the social charade of the gentry's marriage market is played out in the parlour, all beauty and rank sexily on sale to the highest bidder. 'What Brontë does in the pages following Jane's arrival at Thornfield, then, is to reopen the paranoid spaces within an earlier manor house that [Jane] Austen had panelled over with the modern version of English common sense' (Armstrong, 1987:206). Nancy Armstrong's 'paranoia' is my version of adolescent psychology: the gothic playground for psychosocial battles and pacts, seductions and betrayals, transgressions and policings – in struggling to set one's identity in relation to social norms of class, gender, race, generation, etc.

In the scene where Jane first eyeballs Blanche in the parlour, we can see Jane's three purposes intricately at play: defining herself morally by class, regulating her psyche by surveillance and ascetic self-denial, and claiming Rochester's affections by secretly interpreting character, rather than by displaying body and social power – of which she hasn't much, of course. Blanche in the parlour is like Bertha in the attic, a 'third story' who triangulates Jane's self-creation myth. Like Mrs Reed and Mr Brocklehurst, Blanche represents a whole 'story' – script, setting and cast – that Jane could sign up for: the old-fashioned romance. Instead, Jane radically critiques and rewrites the romance while at Thornfield, writing Blanche out and herself in as object of desire, without writing out all grand passion at the expense of common sense. Tricky!

The process occurs psychologically, socially, and materially. In the parlour, Scene One, Jane sneers at Blanche's worn-out romantic notions. Scene Two finds her by the fire with the gypsy, where she has her own self-respecting character and romance 'read' (confirmed by Rochester) as a promise now within her reach. In further scenes with Rochester, Jane is able to 'write' a revised romance, while nightly Bertha savagely satirizes her efforts with uncaptioned gothic illustrations. Jane's remarkable achievement at Thornfield is to nail down a radically *un*romantic marital contract, with herself as wage-earner and unsentimental needler who 'can keep ... in reasonable check' (276) Rochester's angel-slave romantic notions of her. For the off-stage reformation scene, Jane leaves Rochester and Bertha to cleanse themselves of their corrupt (lust and money) marriage, and destroy Thornfield's corrupt charade party with it, returning to Rochester at Ferndean to pick up their contract with even more material equality (if less lust) built in.

Jane's position in Thornfield's parlour as surveillante, manager-of-middle-class-morality, lends considerable evidence to Nancy Armstrong's (1987) theory that novels, beginning with *Pamela*, helped create the character of the middle-class woman as a kind of multipurpose housekeeper. She controls by seeing without being seen, she is valued for her mental rather than physical capacities, and she transforms the hero by changing *his* values from the sexual and material to the spiritual and emotional – that is, from aristocratic to middle-class.

When Jane first hears about Blanche, she draws her portrait as 'an accomplished lady of rank', and her own as 'a Governess, disconnected, poor, and plain', and asks herself which woman Rochester would prefer. 'The contrast was as great as self-control could desire' (*164*). Actually, this exercise in self-governing accentuates her value difference, shows the distance Rochester will have to travel in proposing to Jane, and underlines the victory that a female with an unbuyable 'inward treasure' (*203*) can secure over a female whose expensive estate is 'eligible to the last degree' (*202*). The two portraits are a goad to her psychic self-policing (stay in control!), a set-up for her exposé of aristocratic amorality, and a clear vision of Jane's final social achievement in marrying Rochester.

With her (and our) first view of Blanche thus framed by their difference in social rank, all that Jane sees of Blanche's 'vulgar herd' is easily read as 'faults of her class'. 'Insupportable haughtiness' seems to be an Ingram family trait, though Jane can't see much to be proud of. Lord Ingram is handsome but 'apathetic and listless: he seems to have more length of limb than vivacity of blood or vigour of brain' (*176*). Inbreeding! Blanche has the spirit her family lacks, but it is all demanding and self-centred: 'Whenever I marry', she declares from 'her high horse', 'I am resolved my husband shall not be a rival, but a foil to me. I will suffer no competitor near the throne; I shall exact an undivided homage: his devotions shall not be shared between me and the shape he sees in his mirror' (*181*). Her vision of romance is positively medieval, the woman-as-object courted by the man-as-hunter. 'Loveliness [is] the special prerogative of woman – her legitimate appanage and heritage! ... but as to *gentlemen*, let them be solicitous to possess only strength and valour: let their motto be: – Hunt, shoot, and fight: the rest is not worth a fillip' (*181*). Her taste in romance goes back to pirates, bandits, and gypsies, which is no doubt why Rochester dresses as a gypsy and tells her fortune.

Blanche's aristocratic value, self-described, is her beauty:

'appanage' is 'source of revenue given by a king for the maintainance of a member of the ruling family' (Morris, 1970:62). Since the Ingram estate is entailed to the eldest son, all Blanche's value is, as she says, in her loveliness as an accomplished lady of rank.

Jane's power to see through Blanche transforms all her riches to bankruptcy, because Jane is dealing in another form of currency. Blanche is poor in spirit, and socially 'spends' herself in reckless self-display. While Jane, plain Jane, is a self-made heiress in comparison, hoarding her inward treasure in her screened windowseat. Jane's portrait of Blanche renders her value meretricious, in the original meaning of the word, 'resembling a prostitute', from *merere*, to earn pay, as well as the secondary meaning, 'attracting attention in a vulgar manner' (Morris, 1970:821).

> She was very showy, but she was not genuine: she had a fine person, many brilliant attainments; but her mind was poor, her heart barren by nature: nothing bloomed spontaneously on that soil; no unforced natural fruit delighted by its freshness. She was not good; she was not original: she used to repeat sounding phrases from books: she never offered, nor had, an opinion of her own. She advocated a high tone of sentiment; but she did not know the sensations of sympathy and pity: tenderness and truth were not in her. (*187*)

What a condemnation! So barren a mental soil that nothing grows naturally, and cultivation has only turned up the social surface. Uneducated, Blanche is now uneducable.

Contrast Blanche's character with Jane's – and Rochester does: 'Yes, the future bridegroom, Mr Rochester himself, exercised over his intended a ceaseless surveillance' (*188*). Jane's agonized, yet winning, conclusion is that '*she could not charm him* (*188*). She could not 'influence' him, where Jane sees how 'without weapons a silent conquest might have been won' (*188*). It's all 'inward treasure', girls, what's underneath the social surface, that secret place where, 'though rank and wealth sever us widely, I have something in my brain and heart, in my blood and nerves, that assimilates me mentally to him' (*177*).

'The fine people flitting before you like shapes in a magic lantern' are more like 'mere shadows of human forms, and not the actual substance' (*199*). The popular set, you say to yourself as you watch them dance, are phony. So are prostitutes, and parents, whines Holden Caufield from the American postwar middle class.

Jane, in Rochester's reading, is the real thing, which is of course the protestant ethic. On her face he reads her character – which is, significantly, her future, as middle-class morality promises:

> 'I can live alone, if self-respect and circumstances require me so to do. I need not sell my soul to buy bliss. I have an inward treasure, born with me, which can keep me alive if all extraneous delights should be withheld; or offered only at a price I cannot afford to give.' The forehead declares, 'Reason sits firm and holds the reins, and she will not let the feelings burst away and hurry her to wild chasms. The passions may rage furiously, like true heathens, as they are; and the desires may imagine all sorts of vain things: but judgment shall still have the last word in every argument, and the casting vote in every decision. Strong wind, earthquake-shock, and fire may pass by: but I shall follow the guiding of that still small voice which interprets the dictates of conscience. (*203*)

If Jane's mission at Thornfield is to make romance into realism, make 'the burning clime' a real social world with a place in it for her, her fantasy is now coming true: Romance promises communion and self-knowledge through the other's love. Romanticism promises that truth lies in nature, beyond and underneath meretricious social form – next to the fire, or out in the garden, where Rochester says 'all is real, sweet, and pure' (*217*).

So far, romance *serves* Jane. But when later it appears that Blanche is the winner of Rochester's ring, Jane is able to declare herself free of the silken fetters of desire, and *un*enslaved by love or Rochester: 'I am no bird; and no net ensnares me; I am a free human being with an independent will; which I now exert to leave you' (*256*). This self-assertive declaration of moral integrity critically revises romance and wins Rochester over to *her* class values: '"And your will shall decide your destiny," he said: "I offer you my hand, my heart, and a share of all my possessions.... My bride is here," he said, again drawing me to him, "because my equal is here, and my likeness. Jane, will you marry me?"' (*256*). Possessions aren't the main concessions Jane wants, but rights as an equal whose mental 'likeness' *makes* her equal. This is the feminist (and the middle-class) case for female education, from Mary Wollstonecraft, through Charlotte Brontë, to Betty Freidan and Gloria Steinem. Rochester has proved himself *her* moral equal – apart from his not-so-little secret 'error' in his attic. In recognizing her value he has proven that he is not part of the vulgar herd of the gentry, 'he is not of their kind,' Jane sniffs, 'I believe he is of mine' (*177*).

The trouble Jane has during her engagement with Rochester's sultan–slave romantic script proves that while he may respect the governess's 'still small voice', he none the less has the material means – and accompanying aristo-fantasies – to 'buy' her: 'the more he bought me, the more my cheek burned with a sense of annoyance and degradation' (*270*). Silks and jewels burn like conspicuous consumption through Jane's puritanical heart and temperate body; the psychic associations with Rochester's fallen women are as humiliating as the implied material exchange of body for money. Indeed, the physical is buyable, that's why Jane must insist all value is spiritual.

Marriage gains him possession of her, Rochester says lightly:

> It is your time now, little tyrant, but it will be mine presently: and when once I have fairly seized you, to have and to hold, I'll just – figuratively speaking – attach you to a chain like this' (touching his watchguard). 'Yes, bonny wee thing, I'll wear you in my bosom, lest my jewel I should tyne.' (*272*)

In common law the husband 'covers' all of the wife's legal and economic rights: what was hers is now his. Jane's salary, and her inheritance from Uncle Eyre in the end, are both Rochester's upon marriage, 'special contract' or no. Little wonder Jane finds her future husband's smile one 'such as a sultan might, in a blissful and fond moment, bestow on a slave his gold and gems had enriched' (*271*). Again she asserts her spiritual value over his physical and material terms of possession – 'Don't consider me an equivalent for a seraglio' – *and her right to make her own contract with him*, the essential power Jane Eyre is claiming for middle-class women in marriage. She conjures up a Magna Charta guaranteeing liberty to 'them that are enslaved':

> 'I'll be preparing myself to go out as a missionary to preach liberty to them that are enslaved – your harem inmates amongst the rest. I'll get admitted there, and I'll stir up mutiny; and you, three-tailed bashaw as you are, sir, shall in a trice find yourself fettered amongst our hands: nor will I, for one, consent to cut your bonds till you have signed a charter, the most liberal that despot ever yet conferred.'
>
> 'Why Jane, what would you have? I fear you will compel me to go through a private marriage ceremony, besides that performed at the altar. You will stipulate, I see, for peculiar terms – what will they be?'
>
> ... 'I will not be your English Céline Varens. I shall continue to act as Adèle's governess; by that I shall earn my board and lodging, and thirty pounds a year besides. I'll furnish my own wardrobe out of that money, and you shall give me nothing but – '
>
> 'Well, but what?'
>
> 'Your regard: and if I give you mine in return, that debt will be quit.'
>
> ... 'You will give up your governessing slavery at once.'
>
> 'Indeed! begging your pardon, sir. I shall not.' (*271-2*)

In this haggle over their individual marital contract, we can see that in Charlotte Brontë's version of companionate marriage, material terms dictate who gets a hand in writing the rest of the script. 'Who holds the purse will wish to be master, Ellen; depend on it whether man or woman' (Peters, 1986:192) Charlotte Brontë warned her friend Ellen Nussey. 'I am an independent woman now', Jane tells Rochester before marrying him in the end. Unfortunately, such material independence as Jane Eyre's can be 'written' everywhere *but* in the material world, and there dependence makes very strong claims, especially on one's liberty of mind.

Spiritually, Rochester has uses for Jane too, he says, as '"a very angel as my comforter." I laughed at him as he said this. "I am not an angel," I asserted; "and I will not be one till I die: I will be myself, Mr Rochester, you must neither expect nor exact anything celestial of me ..."' (262). And as for lust – called love or ardour – Jane expects Rochester's to last the usual six months designated 'in books written by men. ... Yet, after all, as a friend and companion, I hope never to become quite distasteful to my dear master' (262). Aristo-passions burn (like Bertha) or bore or betray (like Blanche) themselves away, constancy of character wins the day with Rochester:

> 'To women who please me only by their faces, I am the very devil when I find out they have neither souls nor hearts – when they open to me a perspective of flatness, triviality, and perhaps imbecility, coarseness, and ill-temper: but to the clear eye and eloquent tongue, to the soul made of fire, and the character that bends but does not break – at once supple and stable, tractable and consistent – I am ever tender and true.' (262)

Before leaving Thornfield, Jane has thoroughly revised the terms of romance for companionate marriage. She laughs at the angel wife as a fiction. She declares she'll liberate all women enslaved by love and grant them the right *not* to sell their bodies, and she'll re-educate Rochester as despot until he signs a liberal charter. She'll shop for herself, no doubt for sensible shoes, not be 'dressed like a doll by Mr Rochester' (270). She should have a pretty sexy continental-style honeymoon, if it lives up to the promise of male fiction and Rochester's love does in fact 'effervesce in six months, or less', as advertised. And then, in her fern-covered cottage, as 'a friend and companion', she wants R-E-S-P-E-C-T when she comes home from her hard day's governessing slavery. Sounds reasonable, as far as it goes, although that cottage is described as very damp, and I worry about mould growing on the inanimate and slow-moving.

Thornfield is such fun because it is so removed from anyone's reality; it is – and it is *about* – romantic fiction and the power of reading to bring alive desire. All of Thornfield's characters seem to have read romances, Rochester going heavy on Mme de Stael and George Sand, Bertha clearly a case of overindulgence in gothics, Blanche demanding aristo-porn-romance like Corsair-songs, and Jane a one-plot woman, rereading *Pamela* until 'Mr B' comes round to her point of view. In the field of fiction, heroines can feel, and speak, and set some terms, as Jane does climactically after she works herself up to challenge Rochester on his engagement to Blanche:

> The vehemence of emotion, stirred by grief and love within me, was claiming mastery, and struggling for full sway; and asserting a right to predominate: to overcome, to live, rise, and reign at last; yes, – and to speak. (254)

If romance is about desire, can Jane's revisions of romance then revise women's desire? In romance, the beloved woman becomes mistress of the household if she withstands seduction; Jane's revision insists that it is as a working woman that she'll earn her salary. In romance, the rake is reformed by the love of a good woman; Rochester's turnaround, however, is effected offstage, through God, while Jane's 'conversion' at Moor House makes the religious both personal and political in her power struggle over evangelicism with St John. Thornfield, 'Midsummer Night's Dream' world that it is, is the stage where Jane's feminist power struggles over the terms of romance and marriage and woman's nature engages with the conventions of romantic fiction in its love affair with the Romantic poets.

MOOR HOUSE: EVANGELICISM FOR WOMEN

Waking alone on the cold hillside near Marsh End reminds Jane that the world is not as hospitable as her own literary imagination has furnished it, and indeed is rigidly set in its ways and its places and expectations for Jane. Her encounter with St John has all the inflexibility, claustrophobia, and frostbite induced by an unflinching encounter with reality, with all windowseats barred. In particular, it is an encounter with evangelicism, a considerable religious power in politics and popular debate in England, as in America, in the first half of the nineteenth century. In St John, Moor House, the servant Hannah, and Marsh End, Charlotte Brontë may have punned on three of the most famous and widely published evangelicals of her day: Hannah More, the Marsh family, and John Angell James. Their influential ideas on womanhood offer considerable material for Jane's questioning and cavilling enquiries – and not just for criticism and dismissal, either. The power of the evangelical movement to effect social change, particularly in revising moral relations within the family, had already been proven by 1847, when Charlotte Brontë wrote *Jane Eyre*, and was waning due to the popular influence of secular advice writers like Mrs Ellis, and such literary giants as Dickens, Thackeray, and Tennyson. Secular ideas on a *natural* angelic self-denying womanhood eclipsed an earlier evangelical ideal that was based on the power gained through salvation, which, *Jane Eyre* concludes, offers more truth and power to women in the household. The moral imperative of evangelicism offered women an active agency backed by institutional authority, whereas the vague secular idea of angelic influence was passive and ethereal, even catatonic, in the idealized heroines of Dickens, Thackeray, and Tennyson.

Evangelicism offers Jane a religious foundation to her class-based critique of Thornfield's society set. Conscience supports Jane's refusal of the angel role in Rochester's rake's-reform script, by making him responsible to God for his own salvation. What Jane bluntly dictates to herself forecasts Rochester's physical and spiritual fate and conversion:

> No; you shall tear yourself away, none shall help you: You shall, yourself, pluck out your right eye: yourself cut off your right hand: your heart shall be the victim; and you, the priest, to transfix it. (*300*)

Jane's ice-water conscientiousness at Moor House gives more meaning to the Rochesters' fiery punishments for passion that bring down Thornfield. All the upper-class excesses of character and behaviour that Jane sniffed at from the solitary

From Bad Girl to Good Woman

smugness of her windowseat in Thornfield's parlour, are thoroughly critiqued by evangelicism's superiority of spirit to the vulgarity of money and social status. Religion justifies Jane's class superiority, by claiming to *transcend* all class interest and material consideration. Tricky! And durable: middle-class high culture today rests on its self-announced spiritual superiority – depth of character translated to the truth of art, our secular religion, – in contrast to low culture's and other classes' shallow preoccupations with social and material 'surfaces' (style and stereotypes, B-movies, and graffiti). The rich, the undeserving poor, are poor in spirit; while the aspiring middle class, rising in an expanding economy, is propelled by wings of righteous self-worth. Jane's evangelical rationale for her pilgrim's progress is explained by Davidoff and Hall's description of another heroine's similar rationale, in Jane Taylor's evangelical novel, *Display* (1815):

> Taste and understanding ... were not dependent on money or position but rather on qualities of mind, of reason and culture.... Furthermore, she learnt that it is only religion which can guarantee a true understanding, freed from the trammels of rank, prejudice and party. Real religion required an independence of mind, an ability to go forth on one's own, unaffected by other social interests, with the claims of reason, truth and the spirit to the fore. Religion was the 'one thing needful,' able to free individuals from the patronizing and dependent practices of the old society, able to assert their claim that their 'proud pretensions' stemmed from their faith.
>
> (Davidoff and Hall, 1987:105–6)

Hannah More could quite literally be drawing the moral of Jane's Thornfield escapades, her indulgence in passion, in her *Moral Sketches* (1819):

> Such fascinating qualities are lavished on the seducer, and such attractive graces on the seduced, that the images indulged with delight by the fancy, carry on the reader imperceptibly to a point which is not so far from their indulgence in the act as some imagine.
>
> (Houghton 1957:359–60)

More would agree with Charlotte Brontë that imagination is a seductively strong, restless drawer of bright pictures and whispered of tales to the susceptible – but that is why it is wrong, in More's book, that evangelical bible, Milton's *Paradise Lost*. Seduction exists to be resisted, like the snake in the Garden of Eden hissing in the ear of the all-too-spinelessly-sin-susceptible Eve. More's model wife in her novel, *Coelebs in Search of a Wife* (1807), is, like Milton's Eve, 'obedient and passive, satisfied with influence and with the capacity to inspire male virtues', according to Davidoff and Hall (1987:168).

John Angell James explains why Eve was such a foundation-stone in the evangelical church: 'To be a good wife is a high attainment in female excellence: it is woman's brightest glory since the fall' (Davidoff and Hall, 1987:114). Eve's fallen nature demands all women's salvation through family duty. 'Lack of attachment to a family would mean that women were exposed to being "surplus", with no meaning to their lives, and with the additional dangers of uncontained sexuality' (Davidoff and Hall, 1987:114). There is enough transgressive guilt in Jane to attract her to this view of woman *because it promises purging* of her passions and her solitary uselessness – both weighing on Jane as she crawls towards the light at March End.

John Angell James, nicknamed the Bishop of Birmingham, wrote the most popular religious book after *Pilgrim's Progress*: *The Anxious Enquirer After Salvation*. In *Female Piety or The Young Woman's Friend and Guide through Life to Immortality* (5th edn, 1856), he paints a picture of 'home' as 'the sphere of wedded woman's mission' that rivals Jane's picture of Ferndean for its righteous privatism, its syrupy sentiment, and its use of organic-cultivation metaphors to capture and hide at once the constructed 'nature' of womanhood itself. She implicitly is the 'home' of the family in nature, like a nursery or garden, and a universal centre of gravity and radiation:

> There are few terms in the language around which cluster so many blissful associations as that delight of every English heart, the word HOME. The elysium of love – the nursery of virtue – the garden of enjoyment – the temple of concord – the circle of

all tender relationships – the playground of childhood – the dwelling of manhood – the retreat of age; where health loves to enjoy its pleasures; wealth to revel in its luxuries; poverty to bear it rigours; sickness to endure its pains; and dissolving nature to expire; which throws its spell over those who are within its charmed circle; and even sends its attractions across oceans and continents, drawing to itself the thoughts and wishes of the man that wanders from it at the antipodes: – this, – home – sweet home – is the sphere of wedded woman's mission.
(Davidoff and Hall, 1987:115)

Jane's portrait of Ferdean, her happy family home, is similarly suburban, 'set in the heavy frame of the forest' (*434*). Jane brings the sunshine to the blinded Rochester, when as a mother she restores some vision to his rayless eyes with a first-born son. Jane's use of metaphors from nature to describe her home may have some of her old irony embedded in them, 'deep buried', in the 'dank and green ... decaying walls' (*433*). But maybe not: her Moor House re-education seems to have destroyed her sense of humour.

St John failed to see the humour in his incarnation as God's son on earth, so closely wrapped is his egocentrism. Sainthood was no laughing matter for the real-life John Angell James, who, like St John, 'always enunciated his own thoughts "as if they were absolutely true and incontrovertable", which indeed he believed they were' (Davidoff and Hall, 1987: 128). This is explained by his close identification with God, from whom he gets his orders to subordinate his family:

Every family, when directed as it should be, has a sacred character, inasmuch as the head of it acts the part of both the prophet and the priest of his household, by instructing them in the knowledge, and leading them in the worship, of God; and, at the same time, he discharges the duty of a king, by supporting a system of order, subordination and discipline.
(Davidoff and Hall, 1987:109)

Jane rejects St John's evangelical yoke of wifely subordination, but she does not reject the jobs available to women through his church connections – missionary helpmeet and schoolteacher.

She could have found work (but no pay), as Charlotte Brontë did, in Sunday School teaching, which John Angell James was instrumental in institutionalizing. He organized Sabbath Schools in Birmingham, and the volunteer middle-class women to teach the labouring poor in them. His *Sunday School Teachers Guid* explained how the proper class and gender divisions were to be maintained in them – or, more particularly, how middle-class values were to be enforced *through* them. Here is Jane teaching 'her girls' at Morton School, 'raising them' through literacy and manners, proving herself – and claiming some territory outside the home – as the minister's helpmeet.

At Moor House in St John, Jane comes face to face with evangelicism's contradiction for a woman: her spiritual equality and social subordination. By insisting she'll work with him but not marry him, Jane refuses the lifelong subordination he has in mind for her. From his sisters, however, Jane might have learned a very clever conjuring trick practised by evangelical women on that contradiction.

Female piety was the sticky glue necessary to publicly embrace subordination while privately expanding female domestic power – a female piety subversively reconstituted and reapplied for household use by many ingenious housewives. A mother's responsibility for her children's salvation became, in their hands, the foundation for her moral authority as – dare we say it – head of the household.

Charlotte Brontë's evangelical contemporary Mrs Marsh exemplified this power of female piety, complete in all its ironies, as Charlotte Brontë no doubt would have appreciated. Mrs Marsh's influence came from her death, the absent mother's angelic presence having the last word in the grieving household. Her death left that vacuum where idealization of a minister's wife seems to know no bounds. Her three daughters wrote her memoirs (1837) as instruction manual for her exemplary, secondary-support role. But because such popular memoirs focused on a woman's influence on her deathbed, they 'became the centre of community and family attention, a kind of makeshift pulpit', according to Mary Ryan in her study of evangelicism in Oneida, NY, *Cradle of the Middle Class* (Ryan, 1981:87). 'These deathbed scenes were ... hyperbolic symbols of a new species of woman's influence, the right to hold forth on religious subjects from a position of apparent weakness and to wield the emotional persuasiveness that accompanied these pathetic scenes' (Ryan, 1981:88). The memoirs of Mrs Marsh exemplify the strength-in-weakness evangelical women stole from the church and took home: the domestic power they found for their spiritual equality. With no authority or right to speak within the church, literally no institutional place, evangelical women invested motherhood with all the powers of ministry, a 'vigilant, undistracted watch over a child's soul' (Ryan, 1981:91).

FERNDEAN: JANE'S HOUSEHOLD

Such is the evangelical fire Jane steals from St John and his institutional mission and its secondary place for her, and takes home to Ferndean to establish her own moral authority as mother. 'in 1833 the editor of *Mother's Magazine* put it directly: "The church has had her seasons of refreshing and her turn of decay; but here in the circle of mothers, it is felt that the Holy Spirit condescends to *dwell*. It seems his blessd rest"' (Ryan, 1981:98). Mary Ryan identifies in evangelicism's 'focal point of childhood socialization' the 'linchpin' of change in 'the transition from patriarchal authority to maternal affection' in the middle-class family (Ryan, 1981:102). Jane's powers as a mother and rehumanizing influence on Rochester define Ferndean as home of the new middle-class companionate marriage, triumphant over old patriarchal authorities – dead Mr Reed's will at Gateshead, Brocklehurst's sermons and purse-strings at Lowood, Rochester's romantic lord-of-the-manner-isms at Thornfield, and St John's paternalism at Moor House.

Jane takes from evangelicism the religiously inspired moral authority of motherhood (a kind of immaculate conception from the Heavenly Father), and leaves behind the celibate moral tyranny of paternalism. She leaves St John behind when Rochester calls, but this is not romance calling; it is reformed religion. Rochester calls out at the moment of his conversion, and Jane hears him when she too has entreated Heaven to show her the path, and has been thrilled through with an ecstatic awakening of her senses. Evangelicism is not an end for Jane, but a useful watering hole at which to rethink Thornfield's romance world and sort the delusions and temptations (Blanches and Berthas and gilded prison) from the real substance of *love as moral influence*. What's left is a Rochester blinded to the fleshly and material world, minus his cigar-smoking, whip-holding hand; and an unpretentious cottage instead of a gothic mansion with galloping aristocrats. Jane's romance after her evangelical self-purging is as domesticated as her religion, both patriarchal households gone over with a housewife's keen eye and a mop and broom. All characters outside the cosy circle of the happy couple recede or, provided they're happily married, are invited for a yearly visit. Bertha finishes off Thornfield, and St John finishes off himself, both consumed with that inflammatory appetite that will not contain itself to a fireside at teatime.

Jane's journey from Thornfield through Moor House to Ferndean is the journey of 'Victorian love' itself, its romanticism domesticated by the evangelical family. 'The study of Victorian love', according to Walter Houghton's *Victorian Frame of Mind*:

> is the study of how this [Romantic] tradition, embodied mainly in the works of Rousseau, Shelley and George Sand, was domesticated under the powerful influence of Evangelical and family sentiment, and then emphasized, as a protection against or a solution for, some major concerns of the time: sensuality [Bertha], the marriage market [Blanche], the painful mood of baffled thought, and the decline of religious faith [Rochester].
>
> (Houghton, 1957:375)

The pamphlet Jane picks up from St John's evangelical revival could have been this real pamphlet from Utica, NY, *c*.1823, from Mary Ryan's *Cradle of the Middle Class*: 'A sensible woman who keeps her proper place, and knows how to avail herself of her own powers, may exert, in her own sphere, almost any degree of influence that she pleases' (Ryan, 1981:74). Jane's familiar territory lies in the tension between 'her proper place' and 'her own powers' – a tension apparently resolved by Ferndean's ever-so-simple solution, 'Reader, I married him'.

Is Ferndean an answer to Jane's and the middle-class family's dilemmas? Is a privatized and feminized family – an educated governess wife, 'both prop and guide' to her rehumanized husband, a companionate marriage of remarkable intimacy and equality – *presented as* the solution to all of Jane Eyre's initial questions and cavils about woman's place in the world?

Jane's storybook-simple caption, 'Reader, I married him', is illustrated by her description of Ferndean's fairytale fulfilments in the little house in the big woods. Her conclusion, so simply rendered, was not so simply wrought: rather, it was wrung out of her life at considerable struggle.

Only in fiction lives the happy ending as an automatic part of the natural order of things. Only in fiction does struggle cease upon marriage, and fulfilment settle on the heroine like a profound sleep earned by the working woman's exhausting solitary labour. Only in fiction, where female readers go to be fed, can women demand that their appetites be exclusively catered to, that their ending, the only happy ending, be given them. Our mother, Mrs Rochester, winks as she hands out the ending that readers themselves really write, through their craving for a place where satiety finally rules. Charlotte Brontë impudently stops, in the ending of her last novel, *Villette*, to tell readers to provide their *own* picture of 'union and a happy succeeding life' for the heroine if they want it for her: 'Here pause: pause at once. There is enough said. Trouble no quiet, kind heart; leave sunny imaginations hope. . . . Let them picture union and a happy succeeding life' (Brontë, 1979, 596).

Only in fiction does a heroine's story end with marriage. In autobiography the real story begins in adulthood, when the woman assigns herself the authority to render her life in writing for a public audience. In female fiction, the heroine must marry; we will not put down the book until our demand is met. In female autobiography, the heroine must write. The mystery, the interest, is in how the writer, against all odds, came to write her own story. In Jane's case the suspense is in how the tragicomic plot percolating out of the very raw materials of a ten-year-old Turk of a girl, becomes, in Jane Eyre's capable hands, the triumph of a good woman – and the triumph of a feminist revision of middle-class morality that shows women new means to power in education, romance, religion, and their own households.

I see the ten-year-old Jane Eyre peeking out from behind her red moreen curtain, when the thirty-year-old narrator, Mrs Rochester, announces, 'Reader, I married him'. *She* is the one who discovered at the age of ten that there was no 'natural order' determining her growth into womanhood, no narrative-in-nature ordaining an organic blossoming, and no omnipotent mother or father either, forcing her into a flowerpot against her newly discovered will. This insight, though frightening to behold at such an age – as it was for me at the age of thirteen – is the key to the power of moral agency: the discovered ability to interpret, speak, and act.

Our fiction of a girl becoming a woman weds nature to ritual and conceives a blooming bridal flower. Fictional stories of female adolescence 'speak of ceremony', the pieces written into a 'profound order like natural order'. But autobiography – living and writing the life – is quite another story. Rather than 'something that's just happening', a girl's life at thirteen, like 'Liddy's Orange' in the poem by Sharon Olds, can be ever-so-delicately, juicily, hungrily 'clawed open'.

> The rind lies on the table where Liddy has left it . . .
> All here speaks of ceremony,
> . . . the pieces lying in
> profound order like natural order,
> as if this simply happened, the way her
> life at 13 looks like something that's just
> happening, unless you see her
> standing over it, delicately clawing it open.

(Olds, 1987:74)

BIBLIOGRAPHY

Armstrong, N. (1987) *Desire and Domestic Fiction: A Political History of the Novel*, New York: Oxford University Press.

Austen, J. (1903) *Northanger Abbey* and *Persuasion*, New York and London: G. P. Putnam's Sons.

Brontë, C. (1960) *Jane Eyre*, New York: The New American Library.

Brontë, C. (1974) *Shirley*, Harmondsworth: Penguin Books.

Brontë, C. (1979) *Villette*, Harmondsworth: Penguin Books.

Davidoff, L. and Hall, C. (1987) *Family Fortunes: Men and Women of the English Middle Class, 1780–1850*, Chicago: University of Chicago Press.

Eagleton, T. (1975) *Myths of Power: A Marxist Study of the Brontës*, New York: Harper and Row.

Evans, M. (1982) 'Woman the sufferer: the morality of inequality', unpublished paper delivered at the University of Kent.

Gaskell, E. (1975) *The Life of Charlotte Brontë*, Harmondsworth: Penguin Books.

Gerin, W. (1967) *Charlotte Brontë: The Evolution of Genius*, Oxford: Clarendon Press.

Gilbert, S. and Gubar, S. (1979) *The Madwoman in the Attic: The Woman Writer and the Nineteenth-Century Literary Imagination*, New Haven and London: Yale University Press.

Hall, C. (1985) 'Private persons versus public someones: class, gender and politics in England, 1780–1950', in C. Steedman, C. Urwin, and V. Walkerdine (eds) *Language, Gender, and Childhood*, London: Routledge and Kegan Paul.

Harris, O. (1983) 'Heavenly Father', in U. Owen (ed.) *Fathers: Reflections by Daughters*, New York: Pantheon Books.

Horowitz, H. L. (1984) *Alma Mater: Design and Experience in the Women's Colleges from Their Nineteenth-Century Beginnings to the 1930s*, Boston: Beacon Press.

Bibliography

Houghton, W. (1957) *The Victorian Frame of Mind: 1830-1870*, New Haven: Yale University Press.

Kaplan, C. (1986) *Sea Changes: Culture and Feminism*, London: Verso.

Miller, J. (1986) *Women Writing About Men*, New York: Pantheon Books.

Morris, W. (ed.) (1970) *The American Heritage Dictionary of the English Language*, Boston: American Heritage Publishing Co. and Houghton Mifflin Co.

Newton, J. L (1981) *Women, Power, and Subversion: Social Strategies in British Fiction, 1778-1860*, Athens: The University of Georgia Press.

Olds, S. (1987) *The Gold Cell*, New York: Knopf.

Peters, M. (1986) *Unquiet Soul: A Biography of Charlotte Brontë*, New York: Atheneum.

Peterson, M. J. (1972) 'The Victorian governess: status incongruence in family and society', in M. Vicinus (ed.) *Suffer and Be Still: Women in the Victorian Age*, London: Methuen.

Politi, J. (1982) '*Jane Eyre* class-ified', in *Literature and History* 8 (1): 56-66.

Rich, A. (1979) *On Lies, Secrets, and Silence: Selected Prose 1966-1978*, New York: W. W. Norton and Co.

Rich, A. (1984) *The Fact of a Doorframe: Poems Selected and New 1950-1984*, New York and London: W. W. Norton and Co.

Ryan, M. (1981) *Cradle of the Middle Class: The Families of Oneida County, New York, 1790-1865*, Cambridge: Cambridge University Press.

Showalter, E. (1977) *A Literature of Their Own: British Women Novelists from Brontë to Lessing*, Princeton: Princeton University Press.

Showalter, E. (1985) *The Female Malady: Women, Madness, and English Culture, 1830-1980*, New York: Pantheon Books.

Stoneman, P. (1987) *Elizabeth Gaskell*, Bloomington and Indianapolis: Indiana University Press.

Tannahill, R. (1982) *Sex in History*, New York: Stein and Day.

Taylor, B. (1983a) *Eve and the New Jersualem: Socialism and Feminism in the Nineteenth Century*, New York: Pantheon Books.

Taylor, B. (1983b) 'Freud: father – a poem', in U. Owen (ed.) *Fathers: Reflections by Daughters*, New York: Pantheon Books.

Thomson, P. (1956) *The Victorian Heroine: A Changing Ideal, 1837-73*, London: Oxford University Press.

Uglow, J. (1987) *George Eliot*, London: Virago Press.

Woolf, V. (1978) *Moments of Being: Unpublished Autobiographical Writings*, New York and London: Harcourt Brace Jovanovich.